GOD'S PLAN FOR YOU

by
Keith Butler

Harrison House
Tulsa, Oklahoma

Contents

God Has a Plan for Man

And thine ears shall hear a word behind thee, saying, *This is the way*, walk ye in it.

Isaiah 30:21

Ever since Adam and Eve fell into sin in the Garden of Eden, human history has provided a sad chronicle of man's choices between "truth or consequences." Any honest appraisal of history reveals that *most* of the things suffered by mankind came about because someone somewhere chose to do things *their way* instead of *God's way.*

During my brief stay on this planet, I've seen countless numbers of would-be kings stand on their shaky "kingdom of cards" before TV cameras and reporters, describing how they achieved success or fame in some arena of life. In one way or another, these individuals usually announce with a measure of defiance, "I did it *my way!*"

Very often I see their names show up in obituary columns and news programs announcing their untimely demise and the near-instant collapse of their so-called empires.

The philosophy behind the phrase "I did it my way" didn't originate with any human writer, philosopher or pop singer. It exploded on the earth with the downfall of Lucifer, the egotistical cherubim and arch rebel who thought he could defy the Most High God and subvert His eternal Word. The sad news is that everyone who follows the devil's creed, "I'll do it my way," will end up going his way, following the devil's path to ultimate destruction.

GOD'S PLAN FOR MAN IS ROOTED IN HIS FAITHFULNESS

It doesn't have to be this way. God has a divine plan for man that is rooted in His faithfulness, guaranteed by His eternal Word and undergirded by all of the riches of His glory.

I am saddened when I see research polls declare that they can find no discernible differences between "professing Christians" who regularly attend church and those who know nothing of God. We should see a clear difference between the Church and the world, but it seems we have done our best to "blend in" with the background of secular society.

Christians are just as casual with their use of words as are unsaved people in the world. We know better. We know that God's Word says, "Death and life are in the power of the tongue: and they that love it shall eat the fruit thereof" (Prov. 18:21). Yet even knowing this, we spew out an unceasing stream of negative words that is often tainted with bitterness and will yield an equally bitter harvest in due season.

A large number of nominal Christians have become so influenced by secular thinking that they have set aside God's Word, considering it irrelevant to the modern world. Then they complain that life is difficult because there aren't any guideposts to show them the way.

Our marriages seem to be crumbling just as fast as those of unbelievers, and we wonder why. Our children are rebellious and disrespectful toward any kind of authority, and many have never learned how to handle conflicts safely. They have seen so many murders and rapes on television over the years that they have been desensitized to these crimes and their consequences.

DESPERATELY WANTED: *TRUSTWORTHY* WORKERS

Businesses are at their wit's end. They are desperately searching for employees who are *trustworthy*. Dishonesty, fraud and embezzlement have become common in most workplaces, and some top companies have begun to pay people to train their workers in basic moral values.

America's colleges and universities are turning out an army of highly trained and educated graduates who have virtually no concept of right and wrong, self-discipline or work ethic.

Although these highly educated college graduates come to the workplace with many job skills and qualifications, their employers are asking themselves, "Can they be *trusted* with the assets of this company?" Although they may not realize it, these employers are echoing the concern of the apostle Paul, who wrote, "For I have no man likeminded, who will naturally care for your state. For all seek their own..." (Phil. 2:20,21).

Greed and corruption permeate every level of society and government as an epidemic of immorality is spreading throughout America. We desperately need God's help to escape this trap of our own making.

GENESIS REVEALS PATTERNS AND PRINCIPLES FOR SUCCESS

The first three chapters of Genesis, the "book of beginnings" in God's Word, reveal in microcosm God's plan for man for all the ages. These passages include the first prophetic revelation of the coming of Christ to the earth, and detailed patterns and principles for success in life, marriage, ministry, vocation and human relationships.

No matter how fast or loudly you talk, no matter how skillfully you present your case or repeat your self-justifications, you are headed for trouble if you choose *your way* over *His way.*

Plan on some rough going if you decide to run your marriage your way. You can count on running into serious problems if you decide you are going to date your way or spend your money your way. Grief is inevitable if you decide to have and maintain relationships your way with the people you choose.

Perhaps the most serious consequence of choosing to go our way instead of God's way is that we will find ourselves all alone when trouble inevitably comes *our way* too. God will simply leave it up to *us* to find our own way out of our self-made mess—if there even is such a way out.

As a pastor and church leader, I grow weary of hearing people say, "Where is the Lord in the midst of my troubles? Bishop, I pay my tithes and I go to church every Sunday morning like clockwork. How come I'm not getting any help from God?" Before I can answer, they usually start up again: "Pastor, I just don't understand why this happened to me. Please pray for me."

I Hate To Hear the Eternal "But"

When I ask these people how they landed in their predicament, I usually get an answer that sounds a lot like this: "Well, I know you taught us from God's Word that we shouldn't do this, *but....*"

When I hear the eternal "but," I often interrupt these people to say, "You might as well hold it, because whatever you've got to say after that word 'but' is immaterial." I hate to hear the eternal "but." Honestly, every time I hear people comment on God's Word and then say the word "but," I know exactly "what they fell on"—their "but"!

I'm often tempted to tell these people, "Listen, you dug the hole you fell into, so lay in it for awhile. I'll pray for you after a couple of months." I don't tell them this, of course, but the temptation is strong since people don't always understand their own responsibility for the situations they cause.

YOU HAVE TO KNOW GOD'S WORD TO LINE UP WITH IT

God has revealed His plan for man in the Bible, but you can't align yourself with His perfect plan without studying His Word—and I mean *all of it*. Many Christians have virtually dismissed the entire Old Testament as "no longer relevant." It is no wonder these same people consider the book of Genesis to be unworthy of serious study. *If they only knew....*

I have also noticed that many Christians seem reluctant to study any passage of Scripture or topic on which they have already received teaching in the past. My response is simple: "Did you have steak last month? Did you eat some fried or roasted chicken last week? When was the last time you enjoyed your favorite vegetables or fruits? Does the fact that you had them in the past mean that you will never eat them again?"

Just as you need the basic food groups to daily feed your physical body, so it is with the Word of God. You and I must constantly supply our spirit man with fresh helpings of God's Word in liberal measure.

GOD HAS A PLAN FOR YOU IN PARTICULAR

God's plan for man is revealed at the very beginning of the "book of beginnings," where God describes the creation of the heavens and the earth, and of Adam and Eve. God not only has a plan for man, but He has a plan for *you* in particular.

The basic truth I want you to grasp in this book is this: God's Word is true, and it contains God's plan for all of mankind and for you as an individual. If you search it out and act on God's commands, everything you set your hands to do will be blessed.

On the other hand, you will have problems in life every time you deviate from God's plan and begin to act on your own plan. The logical solution is to find out what God's Word says about life and do things His way.

In the beginning God created the heaven and the earth.

Genesis 1:1

This earth wasn't created by a "big bang" after which everything just "fell into place." Astronomers have determined that if the sun were just a little bit closer to our planet, the heat would literally fry us and make the globe uninhabitable. However, if the earth were to shift from its present orbit even a small distance further from the sun, our planet would soon be uninhabitable because of intense cold.

Earth is home to an incredibly complex and interrelated ecosystem specifically designed to support human and animal life. Everything seems to have its place in God's plan, and the balance in the earth's various ecosystems demonstrates His majesty in creation.

IT TAKES MORE FAITH TO BELIEVE EVOLUTION THAN THE BIBLE

This much I know—our universe and planet didn't happen by accident. Frankly, it takes more unsubstantiated faith to believe the popular evolutionist theories (usually taught as absolute fact) than it does to believe the universe was created as part of a divine plan by a divine being.

> **And the earth was without form, and void; and darkness was upon the face of the deep. And *the Spirit of God moved* upon the face of the waters. And *God said,* Let there be light: and there was light.**
>
> **Genesis 1:2**

The Word of God states in clear terms that the Spirit of God was intimately involved with creation. The Word says nothing about random, meaningless collisions of molecules or matter in space. It says nothing about God preferring to evolve a man from some amoebae in some primordial soup.

The Bible doesn't say that God had to spark life in His creation through a chance stroke of lightning on some floating amoebae in the sea, nor does it say God had to develop man through countless lesser ape-like forms to finally get what He wanted.

LEARN THE PRINCIPLE OF THE "SEED-BEARING SEED"

No, the Creator *created* heaven and earth, and declared that those things He spoke into being were *good.* It is hard to imagine God looking down upon some cosmic collision of lightning and protein in water and declaring such an accidental "creation" as "good."

God removed any doubt about the validity of "species-to-species" evolution when He established the principle of "seed-bearing seed" on the third day.

> **And God said, Let the earth bring forth grass, the herb yielding seed, and the fruit tree yielding fruit after his kind, whose seed is in itself, upon the earth: and it was so.**
>
> **Genesis 1:11**

This principle of "seed-bearing seed" applies to all living things, not merely to the plant world. Even more importantly, this principle applies specifically to the Kingdom of God and especially to "God's seed." This is a principle we must all learn and apply every day of our lives.

God created every species of living thing with the innate ability to reproduce itself. Despite minor adaptations within the species, the ability to reproduce remains intact. You could marry someone of the opposite sex from any race or tribe in the world of man and reproduce "after your own kind."

Pick any apple you like and split it in half. What will you find there? You will find seeds that will produce "after their own kind" if you plant them in soil. People would laugh at anyone who announced they were going to produce oranges from apple seeds, and for good reason. God created all living things to reproduce *after their own kind.*

DISMISS THE THEORY THAT IS NEITHER SCIENCE NOR FACT

The American public school system is devoting a lot of resources to teach the *theory* of evolution as if it were a *scientific fact.* It is neither scientific nor a fact. The idea—and that is all it is—that the human race evolved from monkeys, and ultimately from amoebae in a primordial soup, is only smoke, mirrors and lies. (I have to address this issue because the philosophy under-lying classic evolutionary theory runs contrary to God's Word.)

It is logical to assume that if your uncle is an orangutan then you ought to look like one. I can't speak for your family, but I am absolutely positive that my uncle wasn't an orangutan. My great granddaddy wasn't a knuckle-dragging Neanderthal either.

God created every living thing to produce after its own kind. The proof of this *fact* is all around us. Dogs still produce dogs. Cats still produce cats. People still produce people. In fact, the hundreds of species of monkeys and apes are still producing after their own kind. (Evidently they don't think much of the anthro-pologists who have marked their ancestors as the great "missing link" in evolution between modern man and the monkey world.)

Every living thing was created with the seed within it to reproduce after its own kind. It is significant to me that when God the Creator completed His creative work on the third day, He "saw that it was good."

PLANT THE SEED OF GOD'S WORD

This same principle applies to the *seed of God's Word* in our lives. The Psalmist wrote, "Thy word have I hid in mine heart, that I might not sin against thee" (Ps. 119:11). You must plant the seed of God's Word in your heart to reap a harvest of righteous-ness (and avoid a harvest of grief and sin).

God has a sure plan for man, and the motives behind His plan are beyond reproach. He declares in His Word, "For I know the thoughts that I think toward you, saith the Lord, thoughts of peace, and not of evil, to give you an expected end" (Jer. 29:11). The New International translation puts it this way: 'For I know the plans I have for you,' declares the Lord, "plans to prosper you and not to harm you, plans to give you hope and a future.'"

Yet as good as God's plans are for man—and for you—everything hinges on your willingness to receive His plan and act on it in obedience. The apostle Peter described the works of God in our lives this way (I have emphasized certain key words that apply to this discussion):

> **Grace and peace be multiplied unto you** *through the knowledge* **of God, and of Jesus our Lord,**
>
> **According as** *his divine power hath given unto us all things* **that pertain unto life and godliness, through the** *knowledge of him* **that hath called us to glory and virtue:**
>
> **Whereby are given unto us exceeding** *great and precious promises:* **that** *by these* **ye might be partakers of the divine nature, having escaped the corruption that is in the world through lust.**
>
> **2 Peter 1:2-4**

Success in life (by God's definition) always comes down to the "knowledge" you receive from God and your willingness to live by it.

God has given you "exceeding great and precious promises" in His Word. They are part of His plan for man and for your life. Peter goes on to add that certain things need to be added to your life to make sure you "bear fruit" that pleases God:

> **And beside this, giving all diligence,** *add to your faith* **virtue; and to virtue** *knowledge;*
>
> **And to knowledge** *temperance;* **and to temperance** *patience;* **and to patience** *godliness;*
>
> **And to godliness** *brotherly kindness;* **and to brotherly kindness** *charity.*

> For *if these things be in you,* and abound, they make
> you that ye shall *neither be barren nor unfruitful in the
> knowledge* of our Lord Jesus Christ.
>
> 2 Peter 1:5-8

Peter's message is very similar to that of the apostle James, who wrote, "But be ye doers of the word, and not hearers only..." (James 1:22).

DESTROYED FOR A LACK OF KNOWLEDGE

Any time I see a church, a city, a nation or an individual life fall into decline, I think of the words God spoke through the prophet Hosea: "My people are destroyed for lack of knowledge: because thou hast rejected knowledge, I will also reject thee... (Hos. 4:6).

Although I believe it is rarely productive to point the finger of blame when things go wrong, I am equally convinced that survival requires an honest examination of the problems and mistakes that led to the decline. Much of the time, the problem can be traced to either a *lack of knowledge* or an *unwillingness to apply the knowledge* of God to a situation.

God is a God of order who is never "caught off-guard" by events or the actions of others. He has clearly revealed His plan for man in His Word. Now we must face the same challenge He gave Israel long ago:

> But *the word* is very nigh unto thee, in thy mouth,
> and in thy heart, *that thou mayest do it.*
> See, I have set before thee this day life and good,
> and death and evil;
> In that I command thee this day to love the Lord thy
> God, to walk in his ways, and to keep his command-

ments and his statutes and his judgments, that thou mayest live and multiply: and the Lord thy God shall bless thee in the land whither thou goest to possess it.
Deuteronomy 30:14-16

If there is a "formula" for success in life, then this is God's formula for fulfillment and eternal achievement in life.

GOD GAVE US EVERYTHING WE NEED TO LIVE IN VICTORY

God's plan for man contains wisdom, knowledge and abundant provision for your individual fulfillment as His son or daughter. His plan provides guidance and resources for enjoying life, having a long, happy marriage and raising a healthy, godly family.

He shows us how to overcome every device and attack of Satan, and how we can effectively deal with the desires and weaknesses of "our flesh." God even shows us how to achieve and maintain financial freedom in His prosperity, and how to walk in divine health in our physical bodies.

He has given us everything we need to live victorious and productive lives! "Well, Bishop, I hear what you're saying and I believe it. But will you tell me why my life is in such a mess? Why am I sick all of the time? Why have my finances hit rock bottom and my marriage hit the rocks? Where is God in all of this?"

SEPARATE TRUE FACTS FROM TEMPORARY CIRCUMSTANCES

When you need to understand a thing, you start by sorting out the things you *do not know* from the proven things that *you do know.* Begin your rise from the depths right now by separating the *true facts* in God's Word from the *temporary circumstances* of your life.

As you go through each chapter of this book, measure your convictions, decisions and actions against the *facts* of God's Word to see where you measure up and where you need improvement (we *all* need improvement in places).

I guarantee you that as you acquire the divine wisdom of God found in His Word and put it into practice in your life, you will begin to see the blessing and favor of God fall on your life. Your obedience to His Word will release His abundant blessings on the work of your hands and the words of your mouth.

The Bible isn't merely a book of lofty theology or dusty historical journals—it is the most *practical* "how-to" book ever written, and it was written under the divine inspiration of our Eternal Creator.

The most direct route from where you are today to where you know God wants you to be tomorrow can be found in the road map of the Bible.

God hasn't called everyone to be a Bible scholar, but He *has* called each of us to read and study His Word. It is a lamp, or a light, illuminating life's pathway for our feet. It is our sure guide through the unsure paths of our daily circumstances. It is life-sustaining bread for our hungry souls, and a pool of refreshing water for our heaven-thirsty spirits.

YOU ARE DESTINED TO BE LIKE JESUS

Your destiny, according to God's Word, is to be *like Him:*

But we all, with open face beholding as in a glass the glory of the Lord, are changed into the same image from glory to glory, even as by the Spirit of the Lord.

2 Corinthians 3:18

For whom he did foreknow, he also did predestinate *to be conformed to the image of his Son,* that he might be the firstborn among many brethren.

Moreover whom he did predestinate, them he also called: and whom he called, them he also justified: and whom he justified, them he also glorified.

What shall we then say to these things? If God be for us, who can be against us?

Romans 8:29-31

We are being conformed into the image of Jesus Christ day by day. At times this lifelong process can be painful. Nevertheless, we must learn the ways of God and conform to and operate in them in every way. This is God's plan for man. It is our destiny as the sons and daughters of God.

God's Word says, "If any man lacketh wisdom, let him ask of God, who giveth liberally and upbraideth not" (James 1:5). If you want to discover God's plan for your life, ask Him for wisdom. Seek His face and listen closely for His answer to your prayer.

And thine ears shall hear a word behind thee, saying, *This is the way,* walk ye in it.

Isaiah 30:21

God Creates With Words

And *God said*, Let there be light: and there was light.

Genesis 1:3

We know that the creation of the earth was begun and completed by God over a period of six days, but how did He do it? Did He use some cosmic hammer or ethereal pickaxe? Did He form the mountains and dig the sea beds of the earth with some heavenly shovel or with His own fingers?

Genesis, the "book of beginnings," launches us into our first lesson in "theology" (or the knowledge of God). In the third verse of the first chapter we discover that *God created* light *with words*.

God said it and, instantly, it was. There is a miracle in God's mouth that brings whatever He speaks into existence. "And God said, Let there be light," and there it was. The original Hebrew text says that God literally said, "Light be!" and light was.

I am told that certain scientists came up with the "Big Bang" theory, the idea that the universe was formed by a big explosion hundreds of millions of years ago, because radio telescopes have detected a weak, echo-like signal that is *still* emanating through space. Perhaps this "echo" is actually a lingering remnant of God's spoken command: "Light *be!*"

GOD DOESN'T MAJOR ON THE MINORS

The record in Genesis 1 takes us through each of the six days of creation, painting the cataclysmic events of those moments in broad strokes without regard for specific details. God didn't major on the minors in the first chapter of Genesis. His goal wasn't to chronicle the creation process in exact detail or to provide scientific proof for His own existence.

It seems His chief goal was to drive home a point of eternal importance to His highest creation:

On Day One: *"God said,* let there be light and there was light" (Gen. 1:3).

On Day Two: *"God said,* Let there be a firmament...let it divide the waters from the waters" (Gen. 1:7). God spoke into existence the heavens encircling our planet. The purpose of this "firmament" was to divide the water trapped in our atmosphere from the water pooled and stored in the earth. The next verse tells us, "And it was so."

On Day Three: *"God said,* Let the waters under the heaven be gathered together unto one place, and let the dry land appear: and it was so" (Gen. 1:9).

Having prepared the earth's soil for its first seedtime and harvest, once again that same day, *"God said,* Let the earth bring forth grass, the herb yielding seed, and the fruit tree yielding fruit after his kind, whose seed is in itself, upon the earth: *and it was so*" (**Gen. 1:11**).

On Day Four: "*God said,* **Let there be lights in the firmament of the heaven to divide the day from the night**...*and it was so*" (**Gen. 1:14,15**). **God made the sun, the moon and the stars of the universe and set them in their places. The Word tells us that after God spoke these things into existence and established their boundaries, "God saw that it was good" (Gen. 1:18).**

On Day Five: "God said...." **and the living creatures of the seas and the fowls of the air came into being (Gen. 1:20-23).**

On Day Six: *"God said...."* **and the living creatures of the land, the cattle and the creeping animals appeared on the earth—and then came the creation of man (Gen. 1:24-31).**

Ten times in ten verses in the first chapter of Genesis alone, we read, "And God said...." This may seem a little repetitious to some, but it is clear to me that God is using the power of repetition to reinforce His main point in Genesis 1: *God said, and it was so.*

THERE IS A MIRACLE IN YOUR MOUTH TOO!

How does God create? He does it with words. The miracle of it all is that we are to create with our words too! Not only is there a miracle in God's mouth, but there is a miracle in *your* mouth as well!

The Spirit of God is trying to show us how our Creator operates. Why? It is because God the Holy Spirit, the divine

19

Paraclete who teaches us all things, wants us to realize that *this is how we are to operate too!*[1]

When God breathed the divine breath of life into Adam's lungs, He also endowed mankind with the creative power of speech and declaration. He planted a seed of divine *inspiration,* or breath, within us; and He expects His seed to be a "seed-bearing seed;" as with all other seeds He created. When God says a thing, it comes to pass. *God has the force of faith* because He *believes* that what He *says* is going to *happen.*

Maybe we should too.

God gave the human race, represented in Adam and Eve, the full resources of the earth and the heavens along with a mandate to rule and reign over the earth as stewards over God's creation:

> **And God blessed them** [the first male and female], **and God said unto them, Be fruitful, and multiply, and replenish the earth, and subdue it: and have dominion over the fish of the sea, and over the fowl of the air, and over every living thing that moveth upon the earth.**
>
> **And God said, Behold, I have given you every herb bearing seed, which is upon the face of all the earth, and every tree, in the which is the fruit of a tree yielding seed; to you it shall be for meat.**
>
> **And to every beast of the earth, and to every fowl of the air, and to every thing that creepeth upon the earth, wherein there is life, I have given every green herb for meat: and it was so.**
>
> **Genesis 1:28-30**

Adam was created perfect and without sin, yet he failed. *How can we succeed where he did not?* How can you and I begin to rule and reign in the earth as sons and daughters of God when the world is so filled with sin, pain and lack?

The Spirit of God dwells *within* us and gives us the ability to succeed. God doesn't have to come and walk with you in the garden each morning, because He dwells in your heart every moment of your existence through Christ. You are able to rule and reign in this earth because you do it God's way, *in total agreement with and faith in His Word.*

In addition to God's Spirit dwelling on the inside of us, we also have His Word, which is powerful and sharper than any two-edged sword. (Heb. 4:12). When you speak God's Word in faith, it is as if God Himself is speaking the Word through you.

It is God's Word that cleanses and renews your mind and opens the door for you to operate with the mind of Christ instead of the mind of the flesh.

THE WORD IS YOUR "POWER OF ATTORNEY"

The Spirit of God uses the Word to conform your will to His will, and it is through God's Word that His creative power and ruling authority was delegated to you by Christ through His name. The written Word of God is your legal writ; it is your "power of attorney" and King's commission in writing that certifies your calling and position in Christ. The rest is up to you.

After Jesus' disciples asked Him about the "withered fig tree" in the gospel of Matthew, He tried to explain how powerful faith could be when it is harnessed to the *spoken word,* or released in *prayer.*

The disciples heard Jesus say to a barren fig tree one morning, "Let no fruit grow on thee henceforward for ever"

(Matt. 21:19). When they passed by the same tree later that day, it had already withered away. Jesus answered their question this way:

> **Verily I say unto you, If ye have faith, and doubt not, ye shall not only do this which is done to the fig tree, but also *if ye shall say* unto this mountain, Be thou removed, and be thou cast into the sea; it shall be done.**
>
> **And all things, whatsoever *ye shall ask in prayer, believing,* ye shall receive.**
>
> Matthew 21:21,22

The real key to getting your prayers answered and seeing your professions of God's Word come to pass is simple: *Align yourself with God's Word and purposes before you declare anything.* Then your heart, mind and mouth will be in one accord with the Spirit and Word of God.

FORGET THE MYTH THAT "WORDS ARE JUST WORDS"

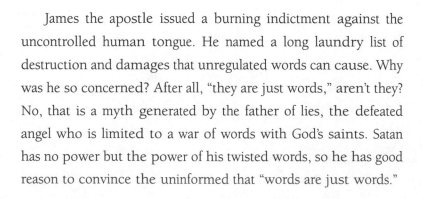

James the apostle issued a burning indictment against the uncontrolled human tongue. He named a long laundry list of destruction and damages that unregulated words can cause. Why was he so concerned? After all, "they are just words," aren't they? No, that is a myth generated by the father of lies, the defeated angel who is limited to a war of words with God's saints. Satan has no power but the power of his twisted words, so he has good reason to convince the uninformed that "words are just words."

James knew that words can release power for good or for evil. He could probably quote the passage from the book of Proverbs that warns:

> **A man's belly shall be satisfied with the fruit of his mouth; and with the increase of his lips shall he be filled.**
> *Death and life are in the power of the tongue:* **and they that love it shall eat the fruit thereof.**
>
> **Proverbs 18:20,21**

James wrote his epistle to Jewish Christians, who had grown up with the Old Testament Scriptures, not to unsaved people. He explained why some of their prayers weren't being answered: "Ye ask, and receive not, because ye ask amiss, that ye may consume it upon your lusts" (James. 4:3).

Beware the "Negative Confession of Faith"

Another error many Christians fall into today involves what I call *negative confessions of faith.* Too many of us have a habit of talking constantly without thinking about what we are saying.

David the Psalmist knew how important it was to guard his words. It was so serious to him that he made it a prayer for all the ages in Psalm 141: "Set a watch, O Lord, before my mouth; keep the door of my lips" (Ps. 141:3).

Jesus Himself confirmed the importance of the words we speak when He issued one of the sternest warnings of His ministry on the earth:

> Either make the tree good, and his fruit good; or else make the tree corrupt, and his fruit corrupt: for the tree is known by his fruit.
>
> O generation of vipers, how can ye, being evil, *speak good things?* for out of the *abundance of the heart the mouth speaketh.*
>
> A good man out of the good treasure of the heart bringeth forth good things: and an evil man out of the evil treasure bringeth forth evil things.
>
> But I say unto you, That every idle word that *men shall speak,* they shall give account thereof in the day of judgment.
>
> For *by thy words* thou shalt be justified, and *by thy words* thou shalt be condemned.
>
> Matthew 12:33-37

We need to seriously examine what comes out of our mouths hour after hour.

Are you complaining, criticizing, gossiping, whining, predicting doom and gloom or spouting doubt and unbelief every waking hour?

Or, are you expressing thanks, lifting up and speaking only good about others, rejoicing, speaking hope and victory over tomorrow and declaring the faithfulness of God and His Word all day long? (It should be obvious which list blesses God the most.)

COME INTO AGREEMENT WITH GOD

We need to avoid the basic errors of praying and speaking in Jesus' name with wrong motives and of speaking negative or idle confessions. If you come into agreement with God in your motives, desires and speech; then the things you speak into the earth on God's behalf will come to pass. They have no choice in the matter, because you are commanding the will of the King of kings!

Does that mean you will not face problems, opposition or failure from time to time? Absolutely not. If you dare to confess that Jesus Christ is Lord and step out by faith to *do something* for Him, you will inevitably hit a "brick wall" of opposition or impossibility someday.

HOW CAN YOU CREATE WITH WORDS?

So how and when can a believer "create with words" as God does? This happens virtually every time you use God's Word to deal with sickness, financial problems, depression or opposition in the workplace or society. It happens every time you obey God's direction to expand a church outreach effort or step into a new area of ministry by faith. You must do what God the Father and God the Son did: Speak the Word.

Whether God is saying, "Light be!" into the darkness at the dawn of creation or speaking a promise of countless descendants over the "nearly dead" bodies of childless Abram and Sarah, we understand from His Word that He "calleth those things which be not as though they were" (Rom. 4:17).

You do the same thing every time you speak God's Word of healing and deliverance over a physical body wracked with pain or debilitated by disease.

When you call for lost souls to be brought in from the north, south, east and west, and when you seek God's face for the salvation of your loved ones and those you meet and work with every day, you are literally *calling those things which be not as though they were!* You are creating a "present reality" with an eternal word in the face of negative, temporary circumstances.

MOVING MOUNTAINS OF SERIOUS NEGATIVE CIRCUMSTANCE

If God calls you into the pastoral ministry or into missions and it means you will have to change careers or even leave your country and home language, you are faced with some serious mountains of temporary negative circumstances. You need a miraculous provision of favor, finances, wisdom and abilities that you just don't have! It is time to begin *calling those things which be not as though they were!*

If you are a young person who knows that God has not called you into a life of celibacy for His purposes, then you need to start off on the right foot right now! There is no better time to start *calling those things which be not as though they were* than *before* you meet your future spouse. Begin to pray for your spouse now—you may not know your future mate's name, home address or how they look, *but God does.* Get involved in their well-being today.

If you are married, but Satan has managed to drive a wedge of division and strife into your relationship with your spouse, you don't have to settle for it. Take authority over the evil spirit that has been dispatched to dissolve your holy union. Speak the Word of God over your spouse and over your home. Don't pray the problem and don't proclaim your emotions over the situation. Pray the Word! No matter how negative your temporary circumstances may be today, begin *calling those things which be not as though they were!*

PRAY THE WORD OVER EVERY SITUATION

If you pastor a local body of believers or are involved in leadership in some way in your local church, you are certain to face challenges and opposition from Satan along the way. No matter what challenge comes against you—whether it comes in the form of resistance from City Hall, persecution from hate groups or opposition from rebellious members of your own fellowship—pray the Word over the situation.

God has a plan for man, and He has a plan for His Body too. It is all found in His Word. Find God's perfect will for each matter that comes up, and begin *calling those things which be not as though they were!*

If you *know* that God has called your local body to build a large facility to better serve God's people and the community, then you also *know* that God expects obedience, and that it can never be accomplished without *faith.*

Begin by *calling those things which be not as though they were!* Don't start with worry or with the busy plans of man. Lay the firm foundation of faith in God's Word—pay no attention to the temporary negative circumstances that seek to deter you from God's will. Everything God births in the souls of men begins and ends in faith, and is built upon the firm foundation of His unchanging, unchangeable Word.

According to God's Word, God does even more than create with His words. The book of Hebrews reveals that God the Son also maintains all things through the power of His word:

> [God] **hath in these last days spoken unto us by his Son, whom he hath appointed heir of all things, by whom also he made the worlds;**
>
> **Who being the brightness of his glory, and the express image of his person, and** *upholding all things* **by the** *word of his power,* **when he had by himself purged our sins, sat down on the right hand of the Majesty on high.**
>
> **Hebrews 1:2,3**

Why do I seem to have such a fixation on God creating with words, on speaking the Word and on walking the walk, not just talking the talk of Christianity?

Jesus rebuked the most religious people of His day, telling them, "And ye have not his [God's] word abiding in you: for whom he hath sent, him ye believe not" (John 5:38). Although Jesus was talking to Jewish leaders who had rejected Him as Messiah, His word also applies to people who "talk the talk" of Christianity but fail to "walk the walk" and live by faith in God's Word.

It is time for God's people to actually live like there really is a God in heaven! We need to walk and talk like God knew what He was talking about, and act like He meant what He said.

THE WORD ISN'T SOME KIND OF
"SPIRITUAL SMORGASBORD"

God's Word isn't a "spiritual smorgasbord." You take it all for what it is—the revealed Word of God, the Truth for all ages, the inspired revelation of God's will—or you reject it all, *and the Lord who inspired and confirmed it!*

The Word, the Bible, is more important than any of us can imagine!

> *The word is nigh thee, even in thy mouth, and in thy heart:* that is, *the word of faith,* which we *preach;*
> That if thou shalt *confess with thy mouth* the Lord Jesus, and shalt *believe in thine heart* that God hath raised him from the dead, thou shalt be saved.
> For *with the heart man believeth* unto righteousness; and *with the mouth confession is made* unto salvation.
> Romans 10:8-10

This divine progression of *belief* with the heart and *verbal confession* with the mouth is God's pattern for all of the Christian life. It isn't merely some protocol for salvation only. Listen to the rest of the message in Hebrews as it describes the role of the Word in our work as evangelists:

> For whosoever shall call upon the name of the Lord shall be saved.
> *How then shall they call* on him in whom they have not believed? and *how shall they believe* in him of whom they have not heard? and *how shall they hear* without a preacher?
> And *how shall they preach,* except they be sent? as it is written, How beautiful are the feet of them that

preach the gospel of peace, and bring glad tidings of good things!

Romans 10:13-15

Everything begins and ends with the Word in God's Kingdom. You believed God's Word after you *heard it*. Once you believed, then you *confessed* it with your mouth.

YOU HAVE A RESPONSIBILITY TO PREACH!

This is what I am trying to say: Once you are a believer, *you have a responsibility to preach the Gospel to others* as an ambassador of Christ—even if you are never called into the five-fold ministry described in Ephesians 4.

God's Word is integral to everything. People come to Christ because they hear the Word and believe. The Word of God is the primary tool we use to help those who already belong to Him become equipped to serve the Lord by teaching them, by training them and to study God's Word for themselves and to share the Word with others.

All of the good things God gives us in life—from our health to our spouses, children, possessions, ministries, relationships or jobs—must then be *maintained* by the Word of His power. This involves *praying* and *speaking the Word* over every key area of our lives.

God's Word tells us that Satan is a liar, and the father of lies. When he tries to bring fear or strife through his lies, we answer with what? The Truth, the Word of God that does not change. We answer every lie of Satan the same way Jesus did—"It is written...."[2]

God Himself chose to *use words* to create the heavens and the earth and all that they contain. We see in His Word that He also continues to *maintain* all that He has created through *"the power of His word."*

The Word of God has made it clear that God has imparted to us the precious *word of faith* to help us walk worthy of our calling in Christ. Our universe and our race began with His Word, our race was redeemed by His Incarnate Word, and we are commanded to live "by every word that proceedeth out of the mouth of God" (Matt. 4:4).

The Word of God simply cannot be overvalued in the Christian life. It reveals God's plan for man, His path for you and the authority we have in this life and will have in the life to come. This is just the first glimpse of what it means to be "made in the image and likeness of God." As I've said before, "The rest is up to us."

C H A P T E R   3

Man: Formed in God's Image and Likeness

**And God said, Let us make man in our image, after
our likeness: and let them have dominion....**
Genesis 1:26

You are made in the very image of God. You are a spirit being
and you have God-like powers in the sense that when you speak,
things come to pass. We have already learned how the words that
you speak have an effect upon you and what happens around you
in the earth as well.

There will be either a miracle or a "mess" in your mouth.
Either way, your words have a key role in bringing about what is
happening around you. Now we will examine how and why this
power was given to us, and then study some specific gender-
based differences embedded in men and women by God Himself
as part of His plan for mankind.

The creation of "man" (*Adam* in the Hebrew) is described
twice in the book of Genesis. The first description is *general* in
nature. In Genesis 1:26, God "in the plural" creates mankind "in the

plural": "And God said, Let us make man in our image, after our likeness: and let them have dominion...."

According to God's Word, God said in the beginning, "Let us...." Who is the "Us" that is involved in creation? We know it wasn't the angels or the demons. If the "Us" in this Scripture passage were only God the Father, He would have said, "I will make...."

We know from the context and from the witness of other Scriptures, such as Genesis 1:2 and the first chapter of the gospel of John, that the "Us" in Genesis 1:26 is composed of God the Father, God the Son and God the Holy Spirit.

"IMAGE" AND "LIKENESS": TWO VERY DIFFERENT THINGS

Secondly, God says something that is crucial to our understanding of His plan for man. He (the Trinity) said, "Let us make man *in our image, after our likeness....*" The terms "image" and "likeness" have two very different meanings.

The Hebrew word for "image" in this passage is *tselem* (tseh'-lem), and it literally means "to shade; a phantom." It is used figuratively to describe our *resemblance* to God in the *inward* sense. Just as God is a Spirit, we were created as eternal spirits too, as spiritual "representations" of our Creator.[1]

The Hebrew word for "likeness" in Genesis 1:26 is *demuwth* (dem-ooth'). It refers to our resemblance in the outward sense. Its focus is upon our physical shape and structure. It describes "what we look like" and "what we are compared to."[2] Family members holding up a newborn child might look at the proud parents and say, "I can see both of you in this baby. He has your eyes, Mama, and he has your forehead, Daddy. He has your likeness (*demuwth*)."

WE LOOK LIKE GOD

So what does it mean to be made in the *"likeness"* of God? The long and the short of it is that we look like God in some way, and God looks like us.

I know that a lot of people have taught over the years that when God's Word talks about God's "mighty arm," His "right hand," or His being seated on a great throne, that these are only anthropomorphic, or man-like, descriptive terms used by men in primitive cultures to "describe the indescribable." I have a major problem with that—Genesis 1:26.

God Himself says we are *made in His likeness*. In addition to that, He consistently uses "anthropomorphic" terms to describe Himself throughout the Bible.

After Moses had spent 40 days in the cloud of God's glory on Mt. Sinai receiving the Ten Commandments and the Law, he asked God to show him His glory. The Lord told Moses that no man could see His face and live, but He promised to do something else for him, and that promise contained one of the most intimate "anthropomorphic" descriptions in the Bible:

> **And it shall come to pass, while my glory passeth by, that I will put thee in a clift of the rock, and will cover thee with *my hand* while I pass by:**

35

> And I will take away *mine hand,* and thou shalt see
> *my back parts:* but *my face* shall not be seen.
> **Exodus 33:22,23**

Keep in mind that this is God speaking directly to Moses. If God isn't supposed to be described in anthropomorphic terms, then somebody forgot to tell Him about it. They keep showing up throughout the Bible from Genesis to Revelation. The reason is obvious judging from what God says in the beginning: "Let us make man in our image, after *our* likeness..." (Gen. 1:26). The Bible isn't saying that God looks like us. It is saying that *we* look like God because He made us that way.

SIN IS THE ONLY THING THAT MAKES PEOPLE UGLY

That means that you are something special to God. You are not ugly or distasteful to Him; in fact as far as God is concerned, there are no ugly people (just as in a the eyes of parents, none of their babies are ugly). Some people may think other people are ugly, but any opinion that differs from God's opinion doesn't matter. The only thing that makes people truly ugly to God and to one another is sin, and thanks to Jesus Christ, that is a curable problem. We are all made in the very likeness of God.

The Bible also tells us we are made in the *image* of God. Jesus told the Samaritan woman at the well in absolute terms, "God is a *Spirit:* and they that worship him must worship him in spirit and in truth" (John 4:24).

God is a Spirit and *so are you.* You are an eternal spirit being who possesses a soul and lives in a temporary physical body. You are not simply a body (although most of the movies, television and radio programs and advertisements in the secular media say that is all you are). You are not simply a soul, which is defined as the mind, the will and the center of emotions.

You are a spirit being, like your Creator. When your spirit finally leaves your physical body someday, the body that is left behind will revert back to dirt if it is left to natural processes.

"HELLO, DIRT"

That is all a human body is: dirt plus a lot of water. Your physical "house" came from dirt. I don't care if it came from white dirt, red dirt, yellow dirt or brown dirt: it is all dirt. Dirt is dirt. Now, I don't recommend that you walk up to your neighbor tomorrow morning with the greeting, "Hello, Dirt!" Nevertheless, your neighbor is a pile of dirt, plus water, plus a soul, and all held together and enlivened by his or her spirit.

That is why any kind of racism—whether it be white racism, black racism, Native American racism, Hispanic racism or Oriental—racism is nonsense. No case can be made for one race being superior to another. In reality, it's all just a lot of dust blowing in the wind.

I CAN ONLY SEE YOUR "HOUSE OF DUST"

The real "you" lives inside your house of dust. You are a spirit who will live forever with "the master of your choice" (Christ Jesus in heaven, or Satan in hell). If you and I met one another at a grocery store or on the street, you wouldn't really see me and I wouldn't really see you. I could only see the house of dust in which you live, and you could only see my house of dust. The reason is that we can only view the natural world through the "portholes" we call eyes.

You are also made in the *very image* of God. This is reflected in what God says about His new creation in Genesis 1:27: "Let *them* (referring to man *and* woman) have dominion." The Hebrew word for "dominion," *radah* (raw-daw'), literally means "to tread down," and it is used to express man's responsibility and power to have dominion, to prevail against and to reign over the earth with God's authority.[3]

God outlined the scope of man's power when He said:

> Let them *have dominion* over the fish of the sea, and over the fowl of the air, and over the cattle, and *over all the earth,* and over every creeping thing that creepeth upon the earth.
>
> So God created man in his own image, in the image of God created he him; *male and female* created he them.
>
> And God blessed them, and God said unto them, Be fruitful, and multiply, and *replenish* the earth, and *subdue* it: and *have dominion* over the fish of the sea, and over the fowl of the air, and *over every living thing that moveth* upon the earth.
>
> **Genesis 1:26-28**

MAN WAS CREATED TO RULE OVER EVERYTHING ON EARTH

God gave mankind, represented in Adam and Eve, total authority over all living things and "over all the earth" (that means that if there had been anything left, it was covered too).

Man was created and empowered to rule and reign over *everything*—everything that crawls, everything that walks, everything that flies, everything that swims and virtually anything that does anything else!

Among other things, that means that mankind is *not* equal with animals or vice versa. Contrary to popular sentiment today, mankind was clearly created to be higher than the animals (the concept of being "politically correct" was unknown then, and will never apply to the things of God anyway).

Mankind has dominion over the animals. As a human being, you are *not* an animal as the anthropologists would have you believe. You may or may not act like one sometimes, but you are not an animal. You are not in the same class with animals because God gave you, as a man or woman, dominion over everything on the earth.

Now, this much is true—our bodies of dust have some similarities with the bodies of animals and even of plants. Modern science has confirmed what the Bible has stated from the beginning—that all living things on this planet were created from the *dust of the earth* in the beginning.

YOUR VALUE AND DESTINY ARE NOT ROOTED IN YOUR "DUST"

A biochemical analysis of the bodies of humans, animals and plants demonstrates that they all share some of the same basic chemical and mineral components common to—you guessed it—*dirt*. Our value and destiny are not rooted in our bodies of dust—they are rooted in our creation as eternal spirit beings made in God's very image.

God in essence made mankind "god [little 'g'] of this world," and commissioned us to exercise *dominion* over everything on the planet. (We will learn in later chapters what happened to mar that picture and what God did to restore it.)

God's original mandate for Adam and Eve is still our mandate today: We are still created in God's own image (male and female), and we are still expected to be fruitful and multiply. We still have the responsibility to replenish the earth, subdue it and have dominion over the fish of the sea, over the fowl of the air and over every living thing that moves on the earth.

The first chapter of the book of Genesis gave us the "peripheral" view, the wide-angle view of how God created man on the sixth day of Creation. The second chapter of Genesis gives us a more detailed "micro-view" of our creation. It is almost as if God wants us to have a minute-by-minute account of our formation because the "small things" are so important to our calling and purpose in His plan.

GOD WAS WAITING ON SOMEONE...

The first thing to notice is that until the time God was ready to form Adam's body, there was very little moisture in the land areas of the earth. It seems as though God was waiting on something or someone. He was. The Bible says:

> These are the generations of the heavens and of the
> earth when they were created, in the day that the Lord
> God made the earth and the heavens,
> And every plant of the field before it was in the
> earth, and every herb of the field before it grew: for the
> Lord God had not caused it to rain upon the earth, *and
> there was not a man to till the ground.*
>
> **Genesis 2:4,5**

Rainfall wasn't part of the original ecosystem for the newly
created earth. If you look closely at the Bible's account of Noah's
day and the great flood, you will notice that God caused water
to descend on the earth from *two* directions at once.

He opened up the "fountains of the great deep" and for the
first time God opened "the windows of heaven" and released
torrential rainfall that lasted 40 days and washed away all of the
polluted race descended from Adam—except for Noah and
his family.

The first time God "watered" the earth appears to be when
He caused a "mist" to rise up and water "the whole face of the
ground" in those moments just before He began to form Adam's
physical body from the dust of the earth.

God gives us a more detailed view of how He created Adam
and then Eve in Genesis chapter 2. It is here that we also learn
about God's plan and intended function for each gender of
mankind in His purposes. The narrative returns us to the sixth
day of creation once again:

> But there went up a mist from the earth, and
> watered the whole face of the ground.
> And the Lord God *formed* man of the dust of the
> ground, and breathed into his nostrils the breath of life;
> and man became a living soul.
>
> **Genesis 2:6,7**

DO YOU FEEL "SQUEEZED"?

The Hebrew word for "formed" is *yatsar*, and it means to "to squeeze into shape or mould into a form like a potter squeezes and molds clay."⁴ So the body of man was pressed, molded, formed and squeezed into shape under the pressure of God's own hands for a divine purpose. Have you noticed that it often takes pressure to create or make something with the ability to handle pressure in its function?

The strongest steel only gains its strength by going through extreme heat and experiencing the stress of equally extreme cooling temperatures.

I understand that diamonds have the same basic carbon molecules found in common coal, but the carbon molecules in diamonds have been crystallized by the extreme pressures and heat stresses under the earth's surface. Without those extreme temperatures and pressure, the carbon molecules would still be dense, common and sought after only for use as a fuel.

GOD DIDN'T BREATHE INTO THE NOSTRILS OF ANIMALS

Once the Lord God formed man from the dust of the ground, the Bible says He "breathed into his nostrils the breath of life; and man became a living soul" (Gen. 2:7). The Bible doesn't tell us God breathed into the nostrils of any animals so they could become "living souls." That is because He didn't—and they didn't. The Master's touch was enough to animate their physical bodies and implant into their DNA all of the instincts so necessary to their survival.

Man could be formed "after God's own likeness" through the same "potter's molding process" which was also used to form the animals. (Gen. 2:19.) That is why the bodies of deceased men and women ultimately break down into the same basic components as the bodies of animals and plants after they are dead.

However, the only way man could be formed in the *image* of God (who is Spirit) was for something special, something unique, to take place.

MAN BECAME A LIVING SOUL

That special *something* happened when God, He who is Life itself, leaned down and breathed His own breath of life into Adam's nostrils. In that instant, man—*Adam* in the Hebrew— "became a living soul."

What happened next seems to have some unique applications to Adam the "man" which do not necessarily pass on to the female who was to be made next.

> **And the Lord God planted a garden eastward in Eden; and there he put the man whom he had formed.**
>
> **And out of the ground made the LordD God to grow every tree that is pleasant to the sight, and good for food; the tree of life also in the midst of the garden, and the tree of knowledge of good and evil.**
>
> **And a river went out of Eden to water the garden; and from thence it was parted, and became into four heads.**

The name of the first is Pison: that is it which compasseth the whole land of Havilah, where there is gold;

And the gold of that land is good: there is bdellium and the onyx stone.

And the name of the second river is Gihon: the same is it that compasseth the whole land of Ethiopia.

And the name of the third river is Hiddekel: that is it which goeth toward the east of Assyria. And the fourth river is Euphrates.

And the Lord God took the man, and put him into the garden of Eden to *dress* it and to *keep* it.

And the Lord God commanded the man, saying, Of every tree of the garden thou mayest freely eat:

But of the tree of the knowledge of good and evil, thou shalt not eat of it: for in the day that thou eatest thereof thou shalt surely die.

Genesis 2:8-17

"THIS IS YOURS—NOW CARE FOR IT"

The area occupied by God's garden called Eden (meaning "delight") was huge. He put Adam in the middle of that fertile expanse and said, "This is yours. Now I want you to dress it and keep it." Adam had a lot of lawn and garden work ahead of him!

It is only *after* these two jobs are given to Adam that we read: "And the Lord God said, It is not good that the man should be alone; I will make him an help meet for him" (Gen. 2:18).

Have you noticed that God gave the first male on this planet two jobs *before* He mentioned providing a companion for him? I believe this is more than an accident—*it is a precedent!* A man isn't supposed to approach a woman about marriage without a job.

GOD MADE MAN TO WORK

A man is *supposed* to have a job, and he is supposed to have *responsibility*. A man is supposed to have something to do before he takes upon himself the responsibility of providing for and caring for a woman as his wife.

My staff and I often counsel young women (and those who are old enough to know better) who tell us, "Well, I'm just in love with that man! He doesn't have a job (those employers just don't understand him), and he doesn't have any money, but we love each other. Isn't that enough? Love is all we need."

I usually shake my head and say, "You can be foolish about this if you want to, and you can also tell yourself that you love each other all you want. That won't change the fact that you can't eat 'love.' And 'love' won't keep you warm in the cold winter wind—you need a warm coat, dry shoes and a weather-tight home. You'd better find a man who has a job!"

A man without a job is an emasculated man. Men need to work. God gave us a crucial clue about the measure of a good man in the book of Genesis: *A man is a man because he has responsibilities.* He is not a "man" merely by virtue of his anatomy—every male mammal created by God can make that hollow brag. Anatomy can only make you male. You can be fifty years old and still be a mere boy when it comes to shouldering man-sized responsibilities and pressures.

WHAT WEIGHT OF RESPONSIBILITY CAN YOU CARRY?

What makes a man a man isn't his physical size or his ability to fight or excel at some physical skill, such as playing basketball, running track or lifting an impressive amount of weight on the bar. The real test of a man is how much weight he can carry in responsibilities, leadership pressures and commitments.

What makes a man a man is his ability to shoulder responsibilities and carry them out faithfully and consistently. True manhood isn't based upon any physical attribute, outward quality or particular age range. See, you can be twenty-three years old and be a man. It is based upon how you take care of responsibility.

A man is responsible. That is why God set a precedent with Adam that says a man needs to know how to get out on his own, accept responsibilities and learn how to take care of himself honorably *before* he assumes those responsibilities for a mate.

Only a foolish woman would marry a man "straight out of his mama's house" before he has learned how to do things for himself. The precedent for safety and wisdom in choosing marriage partners is right there in the Bible! God gave the first man two jobs before He gave him Eve. First God gave Adam some responsibility. Only then would He entrust him with a lifetime mate and companion.

RESPONSIBILITY FIRST, THEN A REWARD

Here is another important concept for men to understand. First you work, then you receive your reward or your pay. Consider what God said to Adam concerning the garden:

> **And the Lord God took the man, and put him into the garden of Eden to *dress* it and to *keep* it.**
> **And the Lord God commanded the man, saying, Of every tree of the garden *thou mayest freely eat.***
> **Genesis 2:15,16**

What is God doing here? He is giving Adam a *reward* or payment for his labor. This is a divine precedent, and it is deceptively simple: You are supposed to get a reward or payment *after* you work. First you work; then you receive your reward. Work brings reward. Where there is no work, there should be no reward.

That is what makes welfare such a terrible thing for people who are physically and mentally able to work. (I believe there *is* a place for charity for those who are sick, infirm or unable mentally or physically to take care of themselves.)

Never Reward Inactivity or Punish Initiative

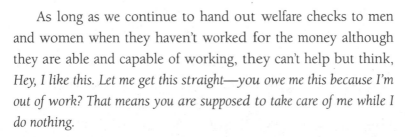

As long as we continue to hand out welfare checks to men and women when they haven't worked for the money although they are able and capable of working, they can't help but think, *Hey, I like this. Let me get this straight—you owe me this because I'm out of work? That means you are supposed to take care of me while I do nothing.*

When a boy sees his father sitting at home day after day with his feet up on the table and a beer balanced on his big round belly, just waiting for another government check to be handed to him after he's done nothing to earn it, isn't it logical to expect that boy to grow up with the same attitude and expectation?

We have an entire generation of young people who believe everything is supposed to be given to them.

"That teacher is just supposed to give me the grades. I ain't supposed to work hard—I'm a basketball player!"

"People are supposed to give me stuff. I ain't supposed to do anything—I'm just a kid from a poor neighborhood."

This kind of thinking and reinforcement of wrong attitudes can cause a complete breakdown of the work-for-reward system God established on Day One of Adam's existence.

GOD IS AGAINST GAMBLING

This should explain why God is against gambling. The whole appeal behind gambling in any form is the idea of getting "something for nothing."

God created man to work for a reward, not to throw the dice and hope chance comes along. Gambling is a sin because it is contrary and opposite to what God has established.

Every time a Christian man steps up to a slot machine, buys a lottery ticket or plays the numbers at the video gambling screen or at the track, he is saying, "I don't believe what God says in Philippians 4:19. I do not believe my God can or will supply all of my need according to his riches in glory by Christ Jesus." He is saying, "God, sorry, but I believe You need some help, so I hope I come up with a lucky...seven!! Give me 25 of those lottery tickets—I've got a feeling God and the state are gonna bless me today...."

God's plan for the male in particular is to work and then receive a reward. "Adam, you get to eat freely from the fruit of the garden and of the tree of life because you have done what I have said." There is something about men that requires them to accept and follow through with responsibilities and work before they can claim true manhood. It is part of proving the "provider calling" with genuine "on-the-job" training before a man can be entrusted to provide for the needs of others who will be *dependent* upon his abilities as a provider and protector. This is God's pattern and plan for the man. Now we will take a look at the "help" who is "meet" for him.

Woman: Made by God's Own Hands

And the rib, which the Lord God had taken from man, made he a woman, and brought her unto the man.
Genesis 2:22

Immediately after God formed Adam's body from the ground and breathed the breath of life into him, He placed him in His garden and put him to work. One of the first things Adam did was name each animal of the field and bird of the air as God brought them to him.

Why was Adam naming the animals when God the Creator had formed them? It was because Adam was the delegated "god" of the world God had created. This man was given all the authority to rule on the earth, so God said, "Whatever you decide to call these animals, that is what they are going to be."

The world Adam discovered in the first day of his existence consisted of three kinds of beings or things. He recognized the first order of being the moment he received his first breath of life from God, the preexistent Creator. In that instant, Adam was fully aware, fully mature and totally equipped for his destiny (although he would soon sense he was missing one very important ingredient).

The second class of created things Adam encountered were those elemental things God *spoke* into existence, such as the sun, the moon, the stars and the land and seas of the earth.

ADAM ALONE RECEIVED THE BREATH OF GOD

Thirdly, Adam became intimately acquainted with the teeming world of "formed" creatures on the land, in the air and in the seas. The bodies of these creatures had also been *formed* from the dust of the earth, but Adam alone had received the breath of God and had been made in God's image and likeness.

As fascinating and as beautiful as the Garden of Eden must have been, God's plan was not yet complete. For the first time in earth's short history, the Creator said that something was *not good*. (Until that time, God had announced that everything He had made and done was "good.") The announcement came after God gave Adam his assignments in the Garden of Eden:

> **And the Lord God said, It is *not good* that the man should be alone; I will make him an *help* meet for him.**
> **And out of the ground the Lord God *formed* every beast of the field, and every fowl of the air; and brought them unto Adam to see what he would call them.**
> **Genesis 2:18,19**

God knew all along exactly what He would do, but He seemed to be making a point to Adam and to all of his descendants who would follow in the centuries to come. Work and communion with God's creation is good and right for a man, but they will never fill the special void God placed in his heart for intimate companionship and completion.

God said, "This bull is strong, but it is not a good companion for Adam. This monkey is mobile and quick in movement and perception, but it isn't going to do for the man. This snake doesn't even come close. I will have to make something that is specially suited just for Adam."

A Unique Creation From Adam's Deepest Core

God's solution was to add one more category of creature to the inhabitants of Eden—a unique creation taken from the deepest core of man's being who would bear the evidence of God's most delicate and refining touch at the culmination of the final day of Creation:

> **And Adam gave names to all cattle, and to the fowl of the air, and to every beast of the field; but for Adam there was not found an *help* meet for him.**
> **And the Lord God caused a deep sleep to fall upon Adam, and he slept: and he took one of his ribs, and closed up the flesh instead thereof;**
> **And the rib, which the Lord God had taken from man, *made* he a woman, and brought her unto the man.**
> **Genesis 2:20-22**

Did you notice that God's Word says He *made* a woman? This is totally different from the way God *formed* the bodies of Adam and the animals. What does this mean?

GOD DIDN'T "SCRAPE THINGS TOGETHER" TO MAKE EVE

The Hebrew word for "made" is *banah* (baw-naw'), and it means "to build, to make, to set up."[1] That means that God didn't scrape together a mound of dirt to begin His work on woman. No, He began with the foundation, the rib of Adam. This was a portion of Adam's skeletal structure that protects the heart and encircles the lungs and the vital organs.

The rib is an encircling bone designed to protect the innermost organs, marked by an amazing level of flexibility and ability to move and expand with every movement of the chest.

Eve, and therefore all of the women who would follow her, have been carefully hand-crafted, specially designed and uniquely customized by God to become the most beautiful thing walking on the planet. That is the woman that God *made*.

God formed the body of man from the ground, the same way he did those of the beasts. But when it came to making the woman, God began with the best of man and went up from there. With His own hands, He rebuilt, remade, hand-crafted and sculpted the woman. (Every man who reads this should shout, "Praise God! I'm glad for that!")

Eve, and every woman descended from her DNA, is special. There is nothing like her. She represents the pinnacle of God's craftsmanship on the final and greatest day of Creation.

FINELY CRAFTED MASTERPIECE: HANDLE GENTLY!

She is a treasure, a finely crafted masterpiece made and meant to be handled gently, attentively cared for and cherished for a lifetime. As the handiwork of God, and made in His image and likeness as was the man, a woman must always be treated properly and with due respect.

There are several important principles revealed in this miracle on the sixth day:

1. When God sees a need in the life of His beloved, if what is needed doesn't already exist, then He will *create* what is needed, and it will be perfectly suited to meet that need.

2. Nothing else would do for man, God's highest creation, than that which was "bone of his bone, and flesh of his flesh."

   God doesn't bless His children with second-best. He blessed Adam with someone who was refined to a higher level than Adam himself.

   He created Adam's "match" using that which was *taken* from Adam's body and spirit (we are not told that God breathed into Eve's nostrils—her life force was the life force God had already placed in Adam).

   Until that match was made, Adam was incomplete by God's design. Adam was still powerful, he was perfectly equipped to lead and rule, but he wasn't complete. He was alone, and that wasn't good in God's eyes.

   The completion that comes through godly marriage transcends mere physical union, and it symbolizes and prefigures an even greater union between the heavenly Bridegroom and His earthly Bride at the great wedding feast of the Lamb.

3. The most important characteristic of women was described by God *before* He made Eve. God *said:* "It is not

good that the man should be alone; I will make him an help meet for him" (Gen. 2:18).

Don't let the Old English terms or the extreme familiarity of this verse fool you. These words are as important today as they were at the dawn of mankind. They describe the nature and purpose behind God's exquisite design of the female human.

The Hebrew word for "help," or helper, is *'ezer* (ay'-zer), and its root literally means "to surround, to protect or aid, to help or succour."[2] (God the Creator even chose a bone from Adam's body that conformed to the meaning of His words!)

The Hebrew word for "meet" is *neged* (neh'-ghed), and it is often translated "suitable." This word literally refers to a "part opposite; specifically a counterpart or mate; usually over against." It comes from a root word that means to "stand boldly opposite, to announce (always by word of mouth to one present)."[3]

God knew what He was doing. He blessed Adam with a beautiful counterpart to surround him with assistance, help, protection and aid.

As Adam's Help *Meet*, Eve Was a Gifted Communicator

Eve was Adam's complementary opposite, the missing part that would complete his identity in the earth. She was the one gifted in one-on-one communication who would be quick to take his part in any discussion or announce his gifts to anyone she met.

She was the one especially equipped to "wrap around him" and adapt to him as if she were molded to his heart and one with his soul.

God created the woman because He knew the man needed somebody. (All the brothers say, "I need somebody.") When God said He would make a help meet for Adam, he was clearly laying out the role of the male and the role of the female in the human race. One of the reasons that we have such chaos in our country today is because we have so much "gender confusion" in our young people.

The confusion doesn't come from God. He has never been confused about the roles, general characteristics and inherent value of males and females. Our society began to drift into confusion when it rejected America's traditional biblical values for the genders in favor of anything *other* than what the Bible says.

Much of the problem stems from absolute ignorance about what the Word of God *really* says and advocates regarding gender roles. The rest comes mostly from outright resistance to ethical codes of conduct and hatred for what is right and good.

GOD DIDN'T ASK ADAM'S OPINION— HE KNEW MAN NEEDED HELP!

God didn't bother to ask anyone's opinion. He just *said,* "It isn't good for this man to be alone. I am going to make a special helper and assisting partner for him." What does that mean? First of all, you should take the hint that *men need help.* (At this point

57

I can always count on some hearty "Amens" from ladies, and some stony silence from men in my audience.)

If you are a man, you must accept the conclusion that God foresaw:

1. You don't *know it all*.

2. You can't *do it all*.

3. You can't *have it all* (when it comes to the intelligence, discernment, abilities and gifts departments).

4. You *need help!*

If God goes to the trouble to make and deliver to you a helper, then you ought to let your helper help you! That is a whole lot easier and wiser than walking around and saying, "Well, I don't need anybody to help me. After all, I'm a man!" That's the point: every man needs help (some more than others).

SHE WAS JUST WHAT HE NEEDED

Another way to put it is that Eve was just what Adam needed. That divine matchmaking didn't stop at the Garden of Eden. You see it all the way through the Bible from Abram and Sarai, to Ruth and Boaz, to Mary and Joseph.

If you are a man and you are married, I can tell you with confidence that based on God's Word, He gave you your mate precisely because she is *different* from you in certain key ways.

She has insights and abilities that you just don't have. She can sense things because God gave her an inner "radar" that is phenomenally accurate. Perhaps you have seen this "radar" in operation already.

A good salesman can come along with a slick brochure and a flaky card, but all you can see is how you'll look driving that vehicle down Main Street or how nice it would be to sit on the deck of that time-share condo that supposedly overlooks prime beach-front property.

All you want to do is kick the tires, check under the hood for obvious oil or water leaks and make the deal. You ask the obviously technical questions about the age of the condo structure and whether or not it has satellite or wide-band digital cable hookups, then you're ready to sign a 30-year contract.

SHE ISN'T IMPRESSED WITH MOUNTAINS OF FACTS AND FIGURES

Husband, you should thank God that your wife functions differently. God gave her an innate ability to sense and see what is going on under the surface of that salesman's slick veneer. She isn't impressed with a long laundry list of facts and figures—she is too busy scanning the eyes and heart for fraud and flakiness.

(The one thing to which she *may be* vulnerable is smooth-talking flattery provided with sensitivity to her needs. Make sure *you* are the one who provides that .)

She can see or sense what you may be totally blind to: "You need to watch this one. Make sure you watch that one right there. Oh, and you had better watch that girl over there." You can't see it. Furthermore, you aren't even thinking about that stuff. As a man, you tend to see something and then do a logical analysis based primarily on the facts presented. If you still like that car, for example, you may buy it on the spot without ever thinking to "check your heart" about the deal.

SHE CAN SMELL THE STINK BEFORE YOU DO

If there is a skunk hiding under that fast talker's outfit, she will smell it out long before you do. You need to listen to her because she will save you a lot of grief, some bumps on your noggin and some real trouble—if you let her.

God gave you someone who is *suitable* and *adaptable* to you. Her chief credentials don't come in an expensive frame from an Ivy League university—she may well have advanced college degrees and enough credentials to wallpaper a bathroom, but her chief credentials are found in her essential makeup.

God gave women the ability to look past the surface details and straight into the hearts and motives of people. Those are the kinds of abilities that are absolutely essential when raising children and running a household; and they do pretty well in every other field of work, service or endeavor too.

Sir, I can tell you this. Your wife and life companion is able to mold and adapt herself to you if she wants to. It doesn't matter how eccentric and strange you may be—chances are pretty good that she read you like a book before she married you. The question is "the want to" part.

WOMEN ARE BETTER AT ADAPTING TO CHANGE

In general, God created the woman to adapt to, help and complete her husband. Many times, a woman may do a far better job than a man when it comes to adjusting to sudden changes, moves or lifestyle adjustments. That is because the woman is to be the one to adapt to be a helpmate to her husband—it is a very special calling that God has blessed her with!

If you are a woman and you are unmarried, you can avoid a lot of unnecessary pain if you notice that after God made Eve, He personally presented her to Adam. Eve did not present herself to Adam; she let God do it. That is another "Genesis precedent" that is still in force today. You need to let the Lord present you to a man instead of trying so hard to present yourself.

Don't scheme and connive ways to "accidentally end up" at the exit he uses at church or the restaurant down the street.

Let God present you to a man. When He presents you, *you are the one!* It is silly for Christian women to be angry at a man for choosing some other woman over her. It really isn't up to the man or to you alone. The Scriptures say:

> **The steps of a good man are ordered by the Lord: and he delighteth in his way.**
>
> **Psalm 37:23**
>
> **Trust in the Lord with all thine heart; and lean not unto thine own understanding.**
> **In all thy ways acknowledge him, and he shall direct thy paths.**
> **Be not wise in thine own eyes: fear the Lord, and depart from evil.**

It shall be health to thy navel, and marrow to thy bones.

Proverbs 3:5-8

I am going to show you in the Bible that when God presents you to a man, you will be a bright light to him. In fact, compared to you, everything and everybody else will be a lesser light.

GOD PERSONALLY PRESENTED THE FIRST WOMAN TO MAN

You already know that God presented the first woman to the first man. It is worth an investment of time to look closely at his hilarious reaction. I have to believe that when God administered the world's first anesthetic to Adam, He told him, "Now, I have something special planned for you, so just lie down here for a minute and let Me take care of business. I can tell you this much, Boy: When you wake up, you are going to say, 'You are my God! I know it!'"

When Adam woke up, he looked at the woman God had made and said, "This is now bone of my bones, and flesh of my flesh: she shall be called Woman, because she was taken out of Man" (Gen. 2:23).

Adam was still in the kingly "name that thing" mode, so he naturally named his counterpart and declared her unique and intimate relationship to him. He was basically saying, "I know what I'm going to call her—woman! In fact, I strongly suspect that when Adam laid his eyes on Eve that he exclaimed, "Whoa—man!"

62

SHE WALKED BY AND THE HEAVENLY HOOK TOOK

How can I be so sure? That is what *I did* when I first saw my wife! There was a whole choir section at that rehearsal containing a number of available women, but I had eyes only for one young woman that night.

She wasn't wearing any makeup and she wasn't all decked out and fixed up like she was "going fishing in the man pool" or anything. She had come to attend a choir rehearsal and she didn't know me from Adam.

I was a seventeen-year-old boy with a hunger for God. When I told a friend that I was looking for a place where people really worshipped God, she named a particular church and I decided to check it out in person.

I was sitting toward the front of the sanctuary when the choir started to march from the back up to the choir loft. As the choir marched by in a single line, I saw an angel in the flesh file past me while singing the praises of God. The heavenly hook took and I said to myself right then and there, *I'm coming back to this church.*

I was in my place and ready to praise that very Sunday. Listen, I understand how Adam felt! It still makes me want to shout, "Glory to God!"

My dear unmarried sister, if you let God do the presenting, your intended groom won't even *try* to run or look elsewhere.

RUTH'S STORY APPLIES TO MODERN CIRCUMSTANCES

The Bible is filled with dramatic love stories and divine match-ups. The story of Ruth is one of the most remarkable because many of her personal circumstances apply in one way or another to many single women in the body of Christ today.

Ruth was a recent widow in the prime of her life, and she knew what it was like to marry someone of another race, religion, culture and homeland. She also knew the bitter language of loss and disappointment. In her day, a widow without a son was in deep trouble.

Things were even worse for her mother-in-law, Naomi, who found herself in a foreign land in her latter years without a husband. When both of her adult sons died, she was left without anyone to help provide for her during her old age.

Logically, Ruth would have had a better chance of landing a husband by staying in her own country with her own people. However, Ruth had married more than a man when she'd married her late husband, Naomi's son. She had married into a God-centered family, and she had grown close to her mother-in-law and had learned to trust in the God she served.

Something deep within Ruth's being told her to stay with her mother-in-law, no matter how foolish it seemed. She left everything behind to follow her Jewish mother-in-law back to Bethlehem in the strange land of Judah. Once the pair had returned to Naomi's native area, Ruth asked permission to "glean," or harvest, leftover grain from some nearby fields, and Naomi agreed. What happened next was *no accident*.

IT "JUST SO HAPPENED" THAT BOAZ PICKED OUT RUTH

If you read through the second chapter of the book of Ruth, you will notice that it *just so happened* that Ruth ended up gleaning grain in a field owned by Boaz, a very wealthy *relative* of Naomi's. It *just so happened* that Boaz decided to make the walk from the city of Bethlehem to that exact field at exactly the time and day that Ruth was working in the field. It *just so happened* that Boaz picked her out from everyone else and everything that was going on at the time and asked his foreman about her.

The fact is that none of these things "just happened." The hand of God was at work in every situation. Boaz nearly fell over himself trying to help this beautiful total stranger. God saw to it that Boaz heard the full report of Ruth's faithfulness to her mother-in-law during hard times. Then Boaz pronounced an amazing blessing over Ruth that reveals the secret of her success in Judah in such a short time:

> **The Lord recompense thy work, and a full reward be given thee of the Lord God of Israel, *under whose wings thou art come to trust.***
>
> **Ruth 2:12**

That prayer set the stage for the rest of Ruth's life in Judah and in history. One comment Naomi made about Boaz seems to sum up what happens to a man who has been introduced by God to the woman he is to marry. Boaz had already promised Ruth he would pursue the necessary channels to marry her, and he sent her home with a generous gift for Naomi.

THE MAN WILL NOT REST UNTIL...

The wise mother-in-law told Ruth, "Sit still, my daughter, until you know how the matter will turn out; for *the man will not rest until he has concluded the matter* this day." (Ruth 3:18.) This is what happens when God does the matchmaking for His children.

Let God introduce you to your future husband. Other women may be doing everything they can to position themselves for maximum exposure and attention, but all they will get from him is, "Excuse me please. You are blocking my view," while he is craning his neck to see *you*. When God does the presenting, that man will have eyes only for you.

(Remember that God won't do this if you have a bad attitude about His timing or methods. God only gives His children good things, and I've never seen a bad attitude classified as a good thing in God's Word.) I am quick to warn Christian men away from "nonadaptive women." I don't consider myself to be an "expert" on women; (I'm just thankful for the wife God gave me. But I do know what God's Word says about choosing a mate. Unmarried Christian men need to run away from a non-adaptive woman because by her attitude she is a prime candidate for becoming what the book of Proverbs calls a "rooftop woman.")

RUN FROM THAT ROOFTOP WOMAN!

God's definition of a nonadaptive rooftop woman is mentioned three times in the Bible. Consider this definition in Proverbs 25:24:

**It is better to dwell in the corner of the housetop,
than with a brawling woman and in a wide house.**

This is the nature of a woman with a serious attitude problem. If you aren't married yet, mister, then it's time to run. Above all, don't get physically close to this kind of woman. Don't let her get your male hormones so heated up that you become oblivious to all of the obvious warning signs until after you say "I do." By then it will be too late.

God created the woman from the very beginning as a divinely designed *help* who was *meet,* or perfectly suited, designed and prepared to help her man, not lead him around by a ring in his nose.

The godly woman is not a doormat, a second-class citizen, a slave or an intellectually inferior human being; but she *is* adaptable, suitable and completing to her mate. She makes everything about him *better* because she is special.

A WOMAN CAN BLESS HER MAN LIKE NO ONE ELSE!

Any honest man of God will quickly admit that he never realized his full potential until his wife "entered the game" of his life. A godly woman can bless a man as nothing and no one else on the planet can, *because God designed her that way.*

As long as she is living and functioning in her role, she is special. If she steps out of her role, she becomes awful. There is nothing worse than a woman trying to be a man (unless it is a man trying to be a woman).

This kind of teaching isn't for people who build their lives according to what the latest television shows are reporting. I'm talking about God's plan, not any man's plan.

These principles from God's Word may not line up with what you were told by your mama, daddy, grandmama or public school teacher. However, they should be life and truth to those people who say that they love and esteem God above all men, and honor His Word as the final authority in all matters.

Finally, it is time to shred some of the myths and falsehoods that have been allowed to bring confusion about what God really says about women and their roles and limitations in society.

THE SKY IS THE LIMIT FOR A WOMAN WHOSE LIFE IS IN ORDER

The truth is that as long as a woman's relationship to her husband and home are in right order, the sky is the limit for her activities and ministry. The proof is in God's Word.

Ruth didn't come from a godly home, and she didn't have much hope for a future. In fact, she came from a group of people called the Moabites who were under a curse of God.

Nevertheless, she did the right thing and chose God over the comforts of her past. He rewarded her with a godly husband who was a wealthy Jewish leader. He gave her a son who became part of the lineage of Christ, who would redeem the entire world.

Esther was essentially an orphan who was raised by her uncle in the capital city of the nation that had conquered her people.

She had little going for her, but God removed the current queen of Babylon and moved Esther into first position as the new queen of Persia—just in time to risk her own life to save her entire nation. She is still considered a revered heroine of the Jewish people, and for good reason.

You are probably already familiar with the remarkable story of *Mary,* the virgin who was chosen to give birth to Jesus, the Son of God; and of *Elizabeth* her cousin, whose once barren womb conceived and gave birth to John the Baptist.

At the same time, God was speaking to an elderly widow named *Anna,* who lived in the temple at Jerusalem. Although by law no woman had been allowed into the presence of God in the Holy of Holies, Anna was destined to look into the face of God Incarnate Himself when she beheld the infant Jesus at the temple.

God honored this woman's faithfulness and blessed her with a glimpse of eternity and the opportunity to prophesy over the One who would redeem all mankind. (See Luke 2:36-38.)

GOD SENT A MAN AND A WOMAN
TO SEE JESUS IN THE TEMPLE

It is interesting to me that God had *a male* and *a female* of the previous generation confirm the identity of His Son when He arranged for Anna and an elderly man named Simeon to meet Jesus' parents in the temple at His dedication. It is fitting that both genders were represented on the day their Redeemer came to the ancient earthly city of God.

From the very beginning of His life on the earth, Jesus—the second Adam—was knocking down barriers for men and women of all classes and stations in life. His life and earthly ministry foreshadowed what Paul the apostle would later declare and seal by the Spirit of prophecy:

> **For ye are all the children of God by faith in Christ Jesus.**
>
> **For as many of you as have been baptized into Christ have put on Christ.**
>
> **There is neither Jew nor Greek, there is neither bond nor free,** *there is neither male nor female: for ye are all one* **in Christ Jesus.**
>
> **And if ye be Christ's, then are ye Abraham's seed, and heirs according to the promise.**
>
> Galatians 3:26-29

CHAPTER 5

Adam's Job Plan
Is Now Your Job Plan

And the Lord took the man, and put him into the garden of Eden to *dress* it and to *keep* it.

Genesis 2:15

What did God do when He put Adam in the garden of delight (which is the literal meaning of "Eden")? Did He just watch while Adam ran among the trees with excitement like someone who has won a shopping spree in a jewelry store? Did He "give him the keys" and tell him to "take a drive" in celebration of his first day on earth?

According to the Bible, God put Adam in the Garden of Eden for a purpose. Man wasn't placed there to become the world's first consumer; he was put there to become the world's first worker—his mission and job assignment was to *dress* and *keep* God's garden.

It is important to understand that every action and decree of God has the potential and probability of being *more* than just a passing event or statement. Many of God's acts and statements in the book of Genesis are intentional *precedents* or *principles* uttered with eternal finality. I believe this is the nature of God's statement about the first man's duties in His garden.

The Bible says, "And the Lord took the man, and put him into the garden of Eden to dress it and to keep it" (Gen. 2:15). Some things never change, and these commands are two of them.

God still wants His children to *dress* and to *keep* His garden, no matter what form it takes in our lives. The One who gave Adam his work assignment is the One who declares "the end from the beginning, and from ancient times the things that are not yet done" (Isa. 46:10). He never intended for His words to fail just because Adam and Eve failed.

What did God mean when He told Adam to *dress* and *keep* the Garden of Eden? Adam "dressed" the garden by working and laboring over the soil and the plants.[1] He had to "till" the land (which included plowing, sowing and raising crops).

LEAD STRAIGHT AND PREPARE FOR SERVICE

To "dress" in this sense can also mean "'to lead straight,' to arrange (as troops) in a straight line and at proper intervals, to prepare for use or service."[2] This reminds me of the apostle Paul's description of the five-fold ministry gifts in Ephesians 4:

> **And he gave some, apostles; and some, prophets; and some, evangelists; and some, pastors and teachers;**

> For the perfecting [straightening and preparation] of
> the saints, for the work of the ministry, for the edifying
> [building up] of the body of Christ:
>
> Till we all come in the unity [single line, single
> purpose] of the faith, and of the knowledge of the Son of
> God, unto a perfect man, unto the measure of the
> stature of the fulness of Christ.
>
> **Ephesians 4:11-13**

If you are not called into a five-fold ministry (and most people are *not),* don't think you are exempt from Adam's job plan. You aren't.

Adam's job plan is now *your* job plan, and it is all part of God's plan for man. What you may not know is that God's assignment to Adam (and to you and me) to *dress* and *keep* His garden reveals two great *success keys* that maximize and ensure the results of the biblical law of sowing and reaping!

DRESS AND KEEP WHATEVER GOD PUTS INTO YOUR HAND

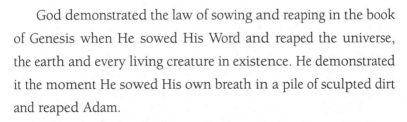

God demonstrated the law of sowing and reaping in the book of Genesis when He sowed His Word and reaped the universe, the earth and every living creature in existence. He demonstrated it the moment He sowed His own breath in a pile of sculpted dirt and reaped Adam.

God also demonstrated the principle of "dressing" when He "tilled," or prepared, the soil and formed it into the shape of a man before He breathed His life into the earthen body.

He has continuously demonstrated the principle of *keeping* by preserving at least a remnant of the human race ever since that sixth day of Creation.

Adam died long ago, but you are still called to dress and keep *the garden of God* in your home, in your marriage, in your parenthood, in your local church and in that part of the lost world that is around you everyday.

God didn't just call you into His family—He handed you a work list with two "chores" on it the instant you received the title of His son or daughter. You are to *dress* and *keep* whatever God puts into your life and hand.

A *KEEPER* GUARDS, PROTECTS, OBSERVES AND PRESERVES

The *second job* God gave Adam (and you and me) was to *keep* the Garden of Eden. The original Hebrew term translated as "to keep" means "to hedge about as with thorns, to guard, protect and attend to. To beware, take heed, observe, preserve, reserve, regard, save and watch."[3]

You should have a very practical understanding of this job. Would you leave your family unprotected and your home and car unlocked and unguarded if you knew a convicted murderer and thief was loose and had been seen in your neighborhood? Absolutely not!

Then why do you do it? Satan is the most motivated, sadistic and evil murderer and thief the world has ever known. Do you raise up the thorny hedge of God's Word in prayer around your family every day?

The Bible says, "Be sober, be *vigilant;* because your adversary the devil, *as* a roaring lion, walketh about, seeking whom he may devour: Whom *resist stedfast in the faith* (1 Peter 5:8,9).

Notice that the Bible does not say the enemy *is* a roaring lion; it tells us he is a pretender who *acts* and *sounds* like a roaring lion. He prefers to strike from the safety of darkness and secrecy, pouncing upon the weak, the unguarded, the unprotected, the unsuspecting and the overconfident.

THE DEVIL HAS NO TRUE POWER OVER FAITHFUL BELIEVERS

The devil has no true power over believers who know and operate in God's Word by faith. It is a different story, however, when believers who know better "fold their hands for a little slumber" and neglect to dress and keep their "gardens."

Even a casual examination of many Christian homes would reveal a picture similar to what Solomon described in the book of Proverbs:

> **I went by the field of the slothful, and by the vineyard of the man void of understanding;**
> **And, lo, it was all grown over with thorns, and nettles had covered the face thereof, and the stone wall thereof was broken down.**
> **Then I saw, and considered it well: I looked upon it, and received instruction.**
> **Yet a little sleep, a little slumber, a little folding of the hands to sleep:**
> **So shall thy poverty come as one that travelleth; and thy want as an armed man.**
>
> **Proverbs 24:30-34**

This is a sad picture of the way many people handle their "God assignments" in life. God is shaking us out of our slumber. He is warning a whole generation of sleepy saints who are snoozing their way through life:

> **Awake thou that sleepest, and arise from the dead,**
> **and Christ shall give thee light.**
> **[Redeem] the time, because the days are evil.**
> **Ephesians 5:14,16**

It is time for us to wake up and align ourselves with God's plan for our lives. This is especially true for men in the body of Christ. God assigned these responsibilities to Adam before Eve was created. At the very least, this means that the duty to *dress* and *keep* should be important to men.

These tasks apply to *everyone* in a general sense, but they have special importance to men because they are intimately intertwined with their purpose and creation as males.

God chose specifically to make this assignment *before* He made Eve and presented her to Adam. He could have waited to deliver the assignment when both the male and female were present, but He didn't.

When Adam Was Ejected, Was His Calling Rejected?

God intended for these duties to be Adam's life calling. Adam and Eve made wrong choices shortly afterward and little further seems to be said specifically about these assignments. I think most people automatically assume those assignments evaporated when Adam and Eve were ejected from the Garden of Eden.

The Bible makes it clear that God doesn't think that way. Consider what He said about His calling and destiny for Israel. He called Israel His "beloved"—even though the Israelites fell into idolatry and apostasy again and again and later rejected Jesus as Messiah. The Bible says, "For the gifts and calling of God are without repentance" (Rom. 11:29).

God knew the man He had formed would soon fall into sin, along with Eve, even as He blew the breath of life into Adam's newly formed body. He wasn't caught off guard or shocked; He had already prepared and anointed a Redeemer to save Adam's descendants from the abyss of sin. The Scriptures tell us Jesus was "the sacrificed Lamb of God" from the beginning of time. (1 Peter 1:19,20.)

My point is that when God told Adam to *dress and keep* His garden, He knew Adam would fail on the job. It didn't stop God from speaking those jobs into existence, because they amount to an eternal job plan for man that applies to every human being who comes to Him.

Eden, the garden of God, is both a literal place and a prophetic symbol representing different "assignments" or gardens of God in the earth. It refers to the earth as a whole, to the human race, to Israel and Judah and to the Church, His prized vineyard and Bride. It also represents *every divine assignment* and God-given responsibility we encounter in our lives. The command to *dress* and *keep* is God's plan for fulfilling our assignments.

"DRESS" AND "KEEP" AT THE SAME TIME

Nehemiah's ministry provides a perfect picture of these activities working together to accomplish the will of God. Nehemiah received permission from Artazerxes, King of Persia, to rebuild Jerusalem's burned out and broken down walls to provide protection for God's remnant people. The only way to get the job done while surrounded by their enemies was to *dress* and *keep* at the same time:

> **They which builded on the wall, and they that bare burdens, with those that laded, every *one with one of his hands wrought in the work* [dressing the walls], and with *the other hand held a weapon* [keeping the walls].**
>
> **For the builders, every one had his sword girded by his side, and so builded.**
>
> **Nehemiah 4:17,18**

JESUS EXTENDED ADAM'S JOB PLAN TO THE CHURCH!

You are probably familiar with the Lord's "Parable of the Talents" in Matthew 25. If you think about it, you may notice that Jesus is actually extending *Adam's two-part job plan* beyond Genesis to every servant of God in the New Testament Church.

Jesus began that parable by saying: "For the kingdom of heaven is as a man travelling into a far country, who called his own servants, and delivered unto them his goods...each according to his ability" (Matt. 25:14,15). He gave one servant five "talents," another two, and a third received one talent.

The first and second servants immediately *put their master's money to work*. The third servant planted his master's goods in a hole of fear and pessimism. When the master returned and asked for an accounting, the contents of this servant's heart were manifested by his words:

> Lord, I knew thee that thou art an hard man, reaping where thou hast not sown, and gathering where thou hast not strawed:
>
> And I was afraid, and went and hid thy talent in the earth: lo, there thou hast that is thine.
>
> His lord answered and said unto him, Thou wicked and slothful servant, thou knewest that I reap where I sowed not, and gather where I have not strawed:
>
> Thou oughtest therefore to have put my money to the exchangers, and then at my coming I should have received mine own with usury.
>
> Take therefore the talent from him, and give it unto him which hath ten talents.
>
> For unto every one that hath shall be given, and he shall have abundance: but from him that hath not shall be taken away even that which he hath.
>
> And cast ye the unprofitable servant into outer darkness: there shall be weeping and gnashing of teeth.
>
> **Matthew 25:24-30**

This is a parable about *the expectations of God.* He gives seed to the sower (that is *you),* and He expects you to plant His seed with faith and believe for a profitable harvest.

God gave you the breath of life so you could preach His Word, praise His name, declare His glory, defeat the devil and prophesy God's will into existence. That is what it means to see God's will "be done in earth, as it is in heaven." (See Matt. 6:10.)

Each of the talents in this parable represents a garden or delightful treasure and investment of God that He has entrusted to men and women once again.

JESUS EXPECTS US TO PLANT HIS MINISTRY FOR A RETURN

When God gave Adam the Garden of Eden, he told Adam to *dress* (till or work) and *keep* (protect and guard) it. When Jesus delivered His ministry to the disciples and the Church after His resurrection, He expected all of us to *dress* and *keep* His garden too. He intends for us to plant His goods and expect an abundant return of like kind.

Unfortunately, a quick scan of many of the churches, leaders and lifestyles of average Christians in America likely would land us in the "hide the one talent" category.

Many of the problems we see in the Church today stem from Christians living as though God saved them so they could "meander through His candy store in an all-you-can-carry bless me" contest. Somehow they never read the Gospels where it says:

> **And he said to them all, If any man will come after me, let him deny himself, and take up his cross daily, and follow me.**
> **For whosoever will save his life shall lose it: but whosoever will lose his life for my sake, the same shall save it.**
> **For what is a man advantaged, if he gain the whole world, and lose himself, or be cast away?**
> **Luke 9:23-25**

Where "the first" Adam failed, Jesus the "second Adam" succeeded. He came to show us how to live and how to die. His life and death are the ultimate proof for the power contained in the law of sowing and reaping. He also showed us how to fulfill Adam's commission to *dress* and *keep* the Father's garden on earth.

SHOUTIN' IS GOOD, BUT FRUITFULNESS IS BETTER

God didn't save your soul, give you a calling or place you in the ministry just so you could have a "shoutin' good time" or feel blessed every time you go to church. Those are wonderful side benefits, but God has a higher purpose and plan for you.

The God who saved you expects you to pick up where Adam left off, to follow where Jesus has set the example: *to dress* and *keep* His garden.

The processes of dressing and keeping a garden show up throughout Jesus' ministry. He stressed the seriousness of a vine dresser's duties in the gospel of Luke:

> He spake also this parable; A certain man had a fig tree planted in his vineyard; and he came and sought fruit thereon, and found none.
> Then said he unto the *dresser of his vineyard*, Behold, these three years I come seeking fruit on this fig tree, and find none: cut it down; why cumbereth it the ground?
> And he answering said unto him, Lord, let it alone this year also, till I shall dig about it, and dung it:
> And if it bear fruit, well: and if not, then after that thou shalt cut it down.
>
> Luke 13:6-9

81

In this parable, the *dresser* of the vines interceded for another chance for an unproductive, unresponsive fig tree. In this sense, Moses was an interceding vine dresser when he interceded for the Israelites and persuaded God not to destroy them for their sins in Exodus 32:31-32.

Abraham was an interceding vine dresser when he interceded for Sodom and Gomorrah, asking God to spare the city if he could find a remnant of just ten righteous men there (Gen. 18:26-32).

THE GREATEST INTERCEDING VINEDRESSER

Jesus is the greatest of all interceding vine dressers. He prayed on the cross, "Father, forgive them; for they know not what they do" (Luke 23:34), and He still continues to intercede for us night and day at the right hand of the Father in heaven. (Heb. 7:25.)

Jesus portrayed the people of His Kingdom as the "salt of the earth" in Matthew 5:13. In that day, salt was the primary preservative used to keep food from spoiling in the Mediterranean heat. God's people as a whole are called to be living, interceding vine dressers who labor day and night to preserve and save the lost.

The God-ordained tasks of *dressing* and *keeping* are so important to the plan of God that Jesus even portrayed the heavenly Father as a "husbandman," or vine dresser, who pruned or trimmed unproductive branches:

> **I am the true vine, and *my Father is the husbandman*.**
>
> **Every branch in me that beareth not fruit *he taketh away*: and every branch that beareth fruit, *he purgeth it*, that it may bring forth more fruit.**

Now ye are *clean through the word* which I have spoken unto you.

Abide in me, and I in you. As the branch cannot bear fruit of itself, except it abide in the vine; no more can ye, except ye abide in me.

I am the vine, ye are the *branches:* He that abideth in me, and I in him, *the same bringeth forth much fruit:* for without me ye can do nothing.

John 15:1-5

Jesus gave us the clearest pattern for "dressing and keeping" every garden God puts in our lives when He prayed His "high priestly prayer" the night He surrendered Himself to the temple guards.

Father, the hour is come; glorify thy Son, that thy Son also may glorify thee:

As *thou hast given him power over all flesh,* that he should *give eternal life* to as many as thou hast given him.

John 17:1,2

In this passage, Jesus describes the "garden" that His Father gave Him, what kind of work He was to do in that garden and the extent of the authority His Father gave Him. He was given all power over the garden of "all flesh," and His task was to "give eternal life" to as many people as His Father gave Him. In the next two verses, Jesus defines what "eternal life" is and declares that He has completed the job:

And *this is life eternal,* that they might know thee the only true God, and Jesus Christ, whom thou hast sent.

I have glorified thee on the earth: I have *finished the work* which thou gavest me to do.

John 17:3,4

83

Jesus used His *Father's words* to accomplish everything in His ministry—especially the things that involved "dressing and keeping" human lives:

> I have manifested thy name unto the men which thou gavest me out of the world: thine they were, and thou gavest them me; and *they have kept thy word.*
>
> Now they have known that all things whatsoever thou hast given me are of thee.
>
> For *I have given unto them the words which thou gavest me;* and they have received them, and have known surely that I came out from thee, and *they have believed* that thou didst send me.
>
> *I pray for them:* I pray not for the world, but for them which thou hast given me; for they are thine....
>
> **John 17:6-9**

God's Word cleans our hearts ("tills the soil"), ignites our faith to confess Christ ("fertilizes our spiritual life"), renews our minds ("lines us up in a straight line"), exhorts us to godliness ("prunes us so we can grow into Him") and equips us for every good work (to bear abundant fruit). All of these functions describe the process of *dressing* the gardens God gives us.

God's Word is also vital to the "keeping" part of our call in God's Kingdom. Jesus describes how He kept those the Father gave Him and how He "sanctified" them, or set them apart, for holy purposes (put a thorny hedge around them):

> And now I am no more in the world, but these are in the world, and I come to thee. Holy Father, *keep through thine own name* those whom thou hast given me, that they may be one, as we are.
>
> While I was with them in the world, *I kept them in thy name:* those that thou gavest me I have kept, and none of them is lost, but the son of perdition; that the scripture might be fulfilled.

Sanctify them through thy truth: thy word is truth.

As thou hast sent me into the world, even so have I also sent them into the world.

And for their sakes I sanctify myself, that they also might be sanctified through the truth.

John 17:11,12,17-19

Results, or "fruit," are the final proof for virtually everything. Jesus warned us in the clear language of a vine dresser when He said, "Either make the tree good, and his fruit good; or else make the tree corrupt, and his fruit corrupt: for the tree is known by his fruit" (Matt. 12:33).

EVIDENCE OF SUCCESS OR FAILURE

All of the things God has placed in our lives or "placed us in" will bear the evidence of our success or failure in *dressing* and *keeping* them.

It takes the hard work of dressing our marriages and children to enjoy the abundant fruit of faithfulness, love, respect and godliness in our homes. It will involve confrontation, correction, repentance and "re-digging the roots" from time to time, but the godly effort you invest in sowing God's Word and into your heart, marriage and home will bear eternal fruit that will bless those who see it. The same is true of your job, vocation or business, and of your ministry or the church you pastor.

What you sow is what you reap; but before you can reap the good things you sow, you must dress and keep it. The only way to *keep* the good things in the "garden" God gave you is to be diligent.

You can't guard, shield and protect precious things by folding your hands and sleeping your way through life. The Word of God is effective only for those who use it like a sword with skill, with Spirit-led knowledge and with the power and force of faith that what God says is true.

God put you in the "garden of the world" for a divine purpose. Your mission and job assignment is the same as Adam's was. You were created, equipped and empowered by God to *dress* and *keep* His garden until His return. Your most important tool for the task is the Word of God, with which you will be able to dress and keep everything He has given to you for His glory.

Free Choice and Earned Consequences

The saga of God's relationship with mankind is a story of choices and limits. God gave Adam the power of choice, and this freedom has been passed down to us as well. We can choose to do whatever we want to do—as long as we are willing to accept the consequences of our choices.

This is what the Lord told Adam after He placed him in the Garden, and just before He made Eve:

> **And the Lord God commanded the man, saying, Of every tree of the garden thou mayest freely eat:**
> **But of the tree of the knowledge of good and evil, thou shalt not eat of it; for in the day that thou eatest thereof thou shalt surely die.**
>
> **Genesis 2:16,17**

God gave Adam *freedom* to eat his fill of *every* tree but one in His garden of delight. The Bible tells us that every tree—that means every single one—in that garden paradise that was probably larger than present-day Iraq and Kuwait put together, was "pleasant to the sight and good for food." (It sounds like the trees of Eden were very different from most of the trees we have today.)

GOD ONLY GAVE ADAM *ONE* LIMITATION

God gave Adam nearly total freedom to eat (and do anything else) as he pleased. According to the Bible, God gave Adam only *one limitation*. He said, "But of the tree of the knowledge of good and evil, thou shalt not eat of it for in the day that thou eatest thereof thou shalt surely die" (Gen. 2:17).

Adam received virtually unlimited blessings and only one limitation. That put the ball back in Adam's court because this meant that Adam would have to *choose* to do right and avoid the one wrong thing in the created world. God's highest creation had been granted the power of *choice*. We still have that power today.

You can choose to serve God, or you can choose not to serve Him. You can choose to believe God, or you can choose not to believe God. (What He says is true, whether or not you are smart enough to believe Him.)

You can choose to do what God says, or you can choose to not do His will, and the only reason you have the power of choice *is because God gave you that choice.*

Why would God the Creator, who possesses all power, choose to give us the right to thumb our nose at Him if we choose to? God gave us the power of choice because He doesn't want robots or automatons.

If He wanted us to obey Him blindly without any choice in the matter, He could and would have made us that way—*but He didn't*. God wants us to follow Him and love Him because we *want* to. He is no different from us, or rather, we are just like Him because we are made in His image and likeness. God, who is Love, knows that true love comes from the heart as a matter of choice and individual will, not through force.

My Wife *Chooses* To Be With Me— This Is Free Choice

I think of this every time I look at my lovely wife. After I thank God for creating me with eyes so I could see and appreciate beautiful things, I rejoice that this woman *chooses* to be with me!

I am larger and physically stronger than my wife, so it is conceivable that I could twist her arm behind her back and ask her in a threatening tone, "Will you love me?" The very thought is repulsive to me, as it should be, but if it happened, she might hesitate to say something so intimate after being manhandled that way.

I could persist and say what some men have been known to say in their more twisted moments, "Say it or I'll break your arm!"

If she finally said, "I love you!" under those circumstances, it still wouldn't do me much good, would it? Why? It is because her confession of "love" was forced against her will and under duress. That isn't love; that is abuse.

On the other hand, if she says, "Baby, I love you," without any pressure, coercion or force from me, then I have been given a high honor. I begin to understand all over again how Adam felt when I hear my wife say, "I love you," from her heart and from her own will. She doesn't have to say that. She could say, "I love somebody else," but praise God, she made a decision to love me!

FREE CHOICE IMPLIES OTHER CHOICES ARE AVAILABLE

Her free choice makes it all the more satisfying because she had many other choices besides me. (None of them were as good as the one she chose, of course.)

God isn't into arm-twisting either. God gave you a choice, just as He has given everyone else free choice in this life. Those who choose to serve Him will, and those who choose not to won't.

That brings us to the limits in life. There are things that are right to do, and there are other things that are wrong to do. God gave mankind the power of choice, but that does not mean that you are the captain of your own ship and that you can do whatever you want, whenever you want. Just forget it! There are limits if you want to receive the blessings of God.

We must all learn about the limits to our freedom of choice. That means you and I must learn how to make good choices and exercise responsibility. This is one of the reasons a man must have a job *before* he begins to court a woman.

If you ever wonder why our society is in such a mess, know that it is because we have never learned to recognize and honor the limits to our freedom of choice, and we don't understand that there are *always* consequences to our choices, whether good or bad.

THE GOOD AND BAD SIDES OF FREE CHOICE

The power of choice has a good side and a bad side to it. It is simple: You enjoy the good benefits every time you make a good choice, and you suffer the negative consequences every time you make a bad choice.

Adam knew better than to violate the one limitation God gave him, yet he did it anyway. In that moment, another principle was revealed as well: The higher you rise in any organization, family or society, the more people will be affected by your choices—for better or for worse.

No matter how much we demand it, dream about it or wish it were not so, God's plan for man does not allow us to live in a vacuum. He created us to weep together, rejoice together and experience birth and death together. That is what it means to be a human being created in the image of the triune God who is One.

DADDY ADAM'S ACTION SET DEATH IN MOTION FOR ALL

Adam was as high as you could get in the human family—he was the "daddy of us all." When he sinned, the consequences of his action set death into motion for *all* of us:

> **And unto Adam he said, Because thou hast hearkened unto the voice of thy wife, and hast eaten of the tree,** *of which I commanded thee,* **saying, Thou shalt not eat of it:** *cursed is the ground for thy sake;* **in sorrow shalt thou eat of it all the days of thy life;**
> *Thorns also and thistles shall it bring forth* **to thee; and** *thou shalt eat the herb of the field;*

**In the sweat of thy face shalt thou eat bread, till
thou return unto the ground; for out of it wast thou
taken: for dust thou art, and *unto dust shalt thou return*.**
Genesis 3:17-19

Verse 19 can easily be bypassed as unimportant by those who
are too familiar with these passages, but it records the actual *death
sentence* that doomed Adam and Eve (and you and me) to physical death one day.

GOD'S PLAN WAS PERFECT—MAN'S PLAN WAS NOT

Death, sickness, disease and lack were never included as
parts of God's perfect plan for man. These are the sad byproducts
of sin, of Adam's fatal choice to seek knowledge and identity
outside of and separate from God's plan.

God never *intended* for a single human being's body to be put
into the ground. He created us to live eternally—even our physical bodies. As I understand it, the cells of the human body appear
to be designed to live *forever.* Scientists have long been puzzled as
to why they gradually run out of energy and die. The answer is in
God's Word in the book of Genesis.

It even appears the animals in Eden never died—or they didn't
until God had to kill two animals and use their skins to cover the
nakedness of Adam and Eve after they sinned. Those innocent
animals died to provide a *covering* for Adam and Eve's shame and
nakedness. This incident marks the first appearance of the blood
sacrifice of innocents as *atonement* for the guilty, and it drives home
the horror of the wages of sin.

The first instance of God *saying something* and it *not* being done occurred after God *gave a limit* to Adam, and Satan challenged Eve about whether God had really said it. In the end, Adam openly disobeyed the one limit God placed on his existence and purpose in Paradise. As a consequence, Adam and Eve were ejected from Paradise and gave up their crowns for the yoke of death.

GOD RISKED EVERYTHING TO GIVE US FREEDOM OF CHOICE

Again, *it wasn't God's choice;* it was man's. It is still that way. Our choices always have consequences. God chose to risk everything by giving us the power of choice in the hope that we would choose *His way* freely and from the heart.

God only gave Adam *one boundary* and countless free choices outside of that boundary. Mankind tends to set up countless boundaries and provide only a few limited choices—especially when God has been removed from the center of their lives.

Where Christ is king, hearts are changed. Therefore, He taught the Jews that only two rules need apply:

> **Jesus said unto him, Thou shalt love the Lord thy God with all thy heart, and with all thy soul, and with all thy mind.**
> **This is the first and great commandment.**
> **And the second is like unto it, Thou shalt love thy neighbour as thyself.**
> **On these two commandments hang all the law and the prophets.**
>
> **Matthew 22:37-40**

93

Where man is king, you need an ever-growing mountain of laws, rules, regulations, limitations, specifications and legal documentation to keep up with all of the vices the human heart can conceive.

God's way—the way of choices plus only the most necessary limitations—is always risky, and it always takes faith. Man's way of extreme choice and no limitations (anarchy), or of extreme limits and few, if any, choices (totalitarianism) *seems* to have few risks, and it takes and allows for no faith. Its end is always the same—death to the spirit.

The Christian life is a life of *relationship* with the living God, not a life of following a book of rules. Once you *know* Him and discover through His Word what He has done for you, you will delight to do His will. It is no burden to live a righteous life in Christ because your love motivates you to please Him in all things.

LOVERS WILLINGLY LAY DOWN THEIR FREEDOM

The Holy Spirit helps us grow into maturity by encouraging us to make *choices* freely according to the truths in God's Word and the voice of the Spirit within our hearts. God always preserves our power of choice, and He delights when we willingly lay down our freedom in order to draw close to Him as our Father, just as lovers willingly lay down their freedom in order to commit their lives to one another in marriage.

Children especially need a healthy balance of choices made within a few important boundaries. This is the pattern we must follow with our children: Give them choices, and give them limits.

If all you give them are choices, they will spend the rest of their lives pressing against authority in all of its forms, seeking the limits they instinctively know are there.

American parents from the "hippie generation" vowed they would raise their children the "liberated way" without correction or limits which might "stifle their creativity." Now many of them know better, but only after they learned the hard way.

Children need to be raised in an environment that has both choices and consequences, but parents have to be strong on both sides of the equation.

The devilish doctrine of secular humanism is based on the thought that you are your own god, and there is no real God outside of what the god-man conceives in his own mind. That is what is being taught to children in many public school curricula.

THERE'S MORE TO EDUCATION THAN THE ABC'S

There have been cases where parents discovered and confirmed that teachers were actually telling their children in the classroom, "Don't listen to your parents. They don't know what they are talking about."

The disconcerting thing about that is that you and I pay hard-earned tax money to help them do that. My friend, there is more to the education process than whether or not your children bring home A's, B's, C's or D's. There is more to it than academics.

Facts and data delivered in a humanistic, anti-Christian context will not produce godly fruit in our children. I would rather have a kid who gets C's and who will live holy, be filled with the Holy Ghost and be anointed of God, than one who gets all A's, is brilliant, but acts like a devil and goes to hell! You can take this counsel to the bank and count on it: If you are going to let your children run with the Philistines, they are going to wind up being Philistines.

The battle for the heart and mind of a child begins and ends in the home. You have to decide whether you want to allow your teenagers to bring the "trash" in from the secular record stores— I'm talking about the kind of music that puts down everything you believe in and promotes everything you do *not* believe in.

"But Bishop, I can't control my kids." How can you call yourself a parent when you don't have any control over your kids? "Yeah, but they are teenagers!" So? That just means they are a little bit bigger than they were two years ago. What do you mean you can't do anything with a fourteen-year-old?

"Oh, Pastor, you're just old-fashioned." No, I'm just speaking the Bible. If that is "old-fashioned," then so be it. Old-fashioned isn't necessarily bad!

I have to tell you that I never raised my voice to my mama because I knew the man of the house would have been there in a minute. I would have been looking up at the ceiling tile. One time at the age of fourteen I thought I was getting pretty big, and independent. My mama's head was considerably lower than my shoulders by then, so I decided to tell her, "Mama, I'm not going to church no more."

I was big, but I wasn't stupid. As soon as I'd said it, I knew enough to know that I had just made a *big* mistake. Mama said, "What did you say to me?" I said, "I'm not going to church anymore." She took a deep breath and turned to face me:

"Let me get this straight. Whose bed linen do you sleep on? In fact, whose bed is it? I don't think it's yours. The clothes on your back—did you pay for them?"

"No."

"Let's see, that fried chicken you like to eat all the time that I bought. Who fixes it? Who cooks it? You don't do it.

"In other words, Boy, as long as you live in my house, you will do what I tell you, or you are going to be out on the street."

When I mention this I can always count on somebody saying, "I can't put my baby out on the street!" My reply is nearly always the same: "Ma'am, your 'baby' knows you feel that way, and that is the reason she will do that! She knows you don't have enough gumption to stand up for your sorry self."

When my mama called my bluff, I knew I wasn't ready to get out there and work for myself and find out what the real world was like. Teenagers don't know what they are talking about most of the time, but it doesn't stop them from *acting* like they do.

When everything is given to them, they think, *Well, this is the way it is always going to be: I am supposed to get a car because I'm here. You are the parent, so you are supposed to take care of me. That means I am supposed to do whatever I want to do.*

EVEN PARADISE HAD ONE LIMITATION

Sorry, it doesn't work like that, because life isn't like that. Even Paradise had one limitation, and my friend, we don't live in Paradise anymore.

I read a newspaper account about officials somewhere in the United States who are attempting to take away parents' right to discipline their kids. The long and short of it is that they want to label everything that speaks of limits and consequences as "child abuse."

There is a genuine problem with child abuse in this nation, and I am sure some Christian parents have been involved in this mess at times. However, most people do not abuse children; they just aggravate the "no limits" crowd because they honor what the Bible says about the value and necessity of *reasonable* discipline. The Bible says:

> **Withhold not correction from the child: for if thou beatest him with the rod, he shall not die.**
> **Thou shalt beat him with the rod, and shalt deliver his soul from hell.**
>
> **Proverbs 23:13,14**

The seventeenth century English terminology may sound a bit rough, but the truth it conveys is eternal and transcends all cultures and ever-changing social fads. God wasn't concerned about being politically correct when He inspired Solomon to write this proverb, and He isn't concerned about it today. He only deals with truth that transcends all things.

"YOU KNOW HOW KIDS ARE..."

I am reminded of the day I walked out of the door of a tailor's shop to find a woman struggling with an eight-year-old boy. This kid was giving the performance of his life. He was throwing himself on the ground and kicking up his legs right there in public.

When his mother tried to pick him up, he slapped her hand and kicked at her in front of me. I watched all of this going on until finally the embarrassed mother looked at me and said, "You know how kids are."

I said, "No, I don't."

It took all of the self-control I could muster to refrain from some vigorous "laying on of hands" that day. I know how kids are, all right. They are born with a sinful nature and they need choices, limits and consequences. That is the Bible way, which means it is *the right way*.

When a small child tries that kind of thing on a Bible-believing parent, it takes about ten seconds for the child to discover that they just crossed the limit and the *consequence* for their action is about to cross their backside. Trust me, that child knows the difference between correction and abuse. They are more likely to believe you love them if you correct them consistently than if you don't.

Unfortunately, many parents (including Christian parents) have been taken in by the people who want to do away with biblical standards of parenting. Many of them wait until their children reach the age of sixteen before they suddenly decide to discipline them.

DO YOU HAVE A FIGHT ON YOUR HANDS?

If those kids have not been consistently disciplined all their lives, then those parents are going to have a fight on their hands. It's too late for reasonable measures. They have to obey or *go* by that stage.

In fact, if anyone lives in your house who is unwilling to follow the rules you establish for your household, *they have to go.* Let them set up their own house, whether they are sixteen or sixty-six.

The problem is that if our children don't learn to live within reasonable limits at home, then they won't know how to follow rules when they get to church, the workplace or the public arena. We run into it all the time in our churches:

The usher says, "Please be seated over here."

"I want to sit over there!"

Or the usher says, "We don't talk in church."

"Well, why not?"

Or, "We don't chew gum in the sanctuary."

"I want to."

We don't talk in the house of God. We praise God. We worship God. We don't visit in the sanctuary. We don't throw paper on the floor.

If you don't learn it at home, you won't know how to do it anywhere else. That is another reason why unmarried Christians need to "observe the tree" of prospective mates—to see if those prospects are bearing the good fruit of self-discipline.

LET THEM HAVE DOMINION

I want you to understand the significance of what God said over mankind in the beginning and why He said it. It has everything to do with where we are today.

God found Himself in a very peculiar position in Genesis 1:26 when He said, "Let them have dominion over the fish of the sea, and over the fowl of the air, and over the cattle, and over all the earth, and over every creeping thing that creepeth upon the earth."

In that moment, God made man the "god" of this world because every created thing on the earth was subservient to him. God also gave mankind (male and female) the power of choice with the opportunity to mess up or to succeed. Given the chance, Adam and Eve messed up.

Adam was essentially given an open-ended lease over the Garden of Eden and the earth during which time mankind would have total authority in the earth. It was an "if/then" agreement, and the "if" part involved honoring God's single limitation.

Adam could yield that authority to others, or he could operate in that authority himself—it was his *choice*. That meant that God was saying, in essence, "I give my man the authority to operate this planet. Go ahead and operate."

A lot of people don't understand this. That is why you hear people on talk shows, in laundromats and in hospital emergency rooms saying, "Well, if God is in control, He's doing a pretty bad job. If He is in control, then why is He allowing earthquakes to shake our cities and kill thousands? Why does God allow floods and hurricanes? Why does God allow war, poverty, child abuse and murder?"

WE WANT TO BLAME GOD FOR
BAD THINGS THAT HAPPEN

The point here is that we want to blame God for the bad things that happen in this life, but God gave the authority of this planet *to man*. He said, "You have dominion over it."

God is supreme, and He is in control, but not in control in the way in which you may think He is. Look closely at what the apostle Paul told the church at Corinth:

> **But if our gospel be hid, it is hid to them that are lost:**
>
> **In whom *the god of this world* hath blinded the minds of them which believe not, lest the light of the glorious gospel of Christ, who is the image of God, should shine unto them.**
>
> **2 Corinthians 4:3,4**

Do you see the phrase "he god of this world"? Notice that the "g" in the word "god" is not capitalized. The reason is simple: That word is not referring to God the Creator. Look at what this "god" is doing, and then ask yourself who or what it is.

This "god" is blinding the minds of people who don't see or hear the gospel so that they can't perceive and receive it. This "god" is doing everything possible to see people sent to hell.

The eternal Jehovah God is in the redemption business, not the damning business. He is in the business of saving, not blinding, people.

The Bible makes it clear that *Satan* is the god (with a *very little* "g") of this world. How did that pretender get this title and authority? It happened in the Garden of Eden the moment Adam

102

and Eve, the gods of the Garden and of the earth, *chose* to follow the serpent's ungodly counsel instead of obeying God's single limitation on their lives.

Jesus didn't challenge Satan's claim to earthly authority when the tempter took Him to a high place and showed Him all of the kingdoms of the earth in a moment of time. The devil said:

> **All this power will I give thee, and the glory of them: for that is delivered unto me; and to whomsoever I will I give it.**
>
> **If thou therefore wilt worship me, all shall be thine.**
>
> **Luke 4:6,7**

Jesus didn't rebuke Satan and call him a liar on this specific occasion because the devil really did have a claim to those kingdoms—Adam gave his planet-ruling authority to Satan through his sin.

What Jesus dealt with was the sinful motive behind the tempter's claims. Satan really did possess those earthly powers at that time, but he had no authority to ask anyone to worship him. Jesus instantly replied with the Word: "Get thee behind me, Satan: for it is written, Thou shalt worship the Lord thy God, and him only shalt thou serve" (Luke 4:8).

In Genesis 2, Satan became god of this world when Adam chose to honor his words over the words and commands of God and lost his divine lease.

Exactly as God had *said,* and exactly the opposite of what Satan claimed, Adam died spiritually the instant he ate of the tree of the knowledge of good and evil. (Gen. 3:6,7.)

Sin instantly separated Adam and Eve from their unbroken fellowship with God, and mankind took on the nature of death. Satan thought everybody in the planet was his servant after that day. The nature of death is in the father, and it passes through the bloodstream to the child. Every human being ever born would be his slave forever because after all, who can be born without a father?

Satan thought, *I've got God now. I've won control of His whole race of people, and they are going to be my servants forever!*

Then God called Adam and Eve and the serpent to stand before Him. First He dealt with the man, then with the woman, and finally He addressed Satan who had taken to operating through the body of a walking, talking serpent:

> **And the Lord God said unto the serpent, Because thou hast done this, thou art cursed above all cattle, and above every beast of the field; upon thy belly shalt thou go, and dust shalt thou eat all the days of thy life:**
> **And I will put enmity between thee and the woman, and between thy seed and her seed; it shall bruise thy head, and thou shalt bruise his heel.**
>
> **Genesis 3:14,15**

Wait a minute, the devil thought. *A woman doesn't have a seed. The man carries the seed. What does God mean by the 'seed of the woman'?*

God was giving a hint to Satan that the seed of the woman was going to regain total authority and was going to bruise his rock-hard head. It was safe to give the devil hints because he doesn't have revelation (and he definitely doesn't know all things, as his Creator does).

All he knew was that something or someone would be coming on a mission from God to do battle with him and that he had better get ready for it! God knew that to have authority in this planet at all, His emissary would have to possess the full range of expression available on this planet. That meant He would have to be *born* here in a human body.

GOD WAS DETERMINED TO MAKE A WAY...

God was hinting at something else that is important for us to know: God was unwilling to allow the man He had made to fall. It didn't matter how foolish or stupid man appeared to be; God was determined to make a way.

It would take another Adam, another "firstborn" of a different order, with the determination to make a life-threatening *right choice* that would reverse the curse of the Adam who had made a fatal *wrong choice*. Satan didn't know it, but the first Christmas was just around the corner.

C H A P T E R   7

God's Plan for Ignorance:
How To Avoid the Devil's Tricks and Traps

Satan is the most dangerous con artist and swindler of all time, but many people don't realize he is unable to change his tactics. He has been pulling the same old tricks in the same old way for all the 6,000 years that men have been on this planet. *He hasn't changed.*

As I've said before, God has a far-reaching and comprehensive plan for man. He has a clear-cut purpose for all of us, for each gender and for each individual. He even has a plan for "ignorance."

Paul the apostle wrote to the church at Corinth: "To whom ye forgive any thing, I forgive also...lest Satan should get an advantage of us: for we are not *ignorant* of his devices (2 Cor. 2:10,11).

Have we as God's people digressed since Paul's day? I hope not, but there does seem to be a great deal of ignorance in the body of Christ where Satan's devices are concerned. If it isn't true, at least it looks that way because so many of us keep falling for the same old tricks of Satan over and over again.

Paul said we should not be ignorant of Satan's devices because that snake has not changed his tactics since he pulled a "bait and switch" in the Garden of Eden.

According to the apostle Paul, the best defense against the schemes of the enemy is to be aware of his techniques and tricks. You won't fall for his devices when you understand how he operates and how he comes against you.

SATAN'S FAVORITE BAIT WORKS JUST A LITTLE TOO WELL

Satan is a lot like an old fisherman who only has a few favorite baits in his tackle box. He is too old and limited to come up with new baits and fishing techniques, but he sure knows the habits and weaknesses of the fish in his fishing hole. His old favorites work just a little too well on born-again Christians. That means that Hosea's prophetic warning is true once more: "My people are destroyed for lack of knowledge."

The tempter is still pulling the same tricks on you and me that he used long ago to entrap the first woman and the first man. That means we need to identify those things so we can operate in God's plan and not fall for Satan's schemes. The search begins at the beginning, again in the book of Genesis:

> **Now the serpent was more subtle than any beast of the field which the Lord God had made. And he said *unto the woman*, Yea, *hath God said*, Ye shall not eat of every tree of the garden?**
>
> **Genesis 3:1**

Notice that the enemy of our souls never seems to attack "from the front." He begins with an assault to the side by approaching the woman God made from Adam's rib.

If you must defeat a two-person team, you rarely begin with an assault on the strongest or senior member. You tackle the junior or smaller member first, hoping to divide and conquer. This technique began with Satan in the Garden.

THE FIRST DEVILISH DEVICE: INTRODUCE DOUBT

Satan's *"first device"* is to question God's Word in a *subtle* way. "Hath God said...?" The devil always works to introduce doubt, but usually he does it so smoothly that you may not even recognize it at first. He is still using the same technique he used on Eve in the Garden of Eden:

> **Now the serpent was more subtle than any beast of the field which the Lord God had made. And he said unto the woman, Yea, hath God said, Ye shall not eat of every tree of the garden?**
>
> **Genesis 3:1**

The Hebrew word for "subtle" in this passage means "cunning, crafty and smooth."[1] The more you understand the deceiver's ways, the more you will see that he likes to "ask questions," which is really his means of planting "doubt darts" in our hearts and minds: *"Is it really this way? Did God really mean what He said? Come on now...does it really have to be this way and this way only? You know, I feel like it should be understood this way. What did God really say about this matter?"*

109

It was no accident that Satan "asked" Eve, "Hath God said..." He wasn't interested in Eve's answer, he was interested in planting his own answer in Eve's mind. He purposely *misquoted* God's words in the negative. That required Eve to repeat the second-hand version of Adam's conversation with God—a conversation that took place before she was created.

The enemy's pattern is simple. America's trial attorneys use the same technique in our courtrooms every day. First you introduce doubt about a person's accuracy as a listener and as a witness by picking apart the details of their testimony. Then you establish *your* credibility *while introducing doubt about the accuracy of the original source*. This is how Satan did it in the Garden that day:

> **And he said unto the woman, Yea, *hath God said*, Ye shall not eat of every tree of the garden?**
> **And the woman said unto the serpent, We may eat of the fruit of the trees of the garden:**
> **But of the fruit of the tree which is in the midst of the garden, God hath said, Ye shall not eat of it, neither shall ye touch it, lest ye die.**
>
> **Genesis 3:1-3**

We know from Genesis 2 that God talked directly with Adam about these things before He ever created Eve. How, then, did she find out about this conversation? The answer is simple: Adam told her.

God actually told Adam, "But of the tree of the knowledge of good and evil, thou shalt not eat of it: for in the day that thou eatest thereof thou shalt surely die" (Gen. 2:17).

Eve's version went like this: "But of the fruit of the tree which is in the midst of the garden, God hath said, ye shall not eat of it, neither shall ye touch it, lest ye die" (Gen. 3:3).

Her husband must have expounded a little on God's words for added effect: "Eve, don't you even *look* at that tree. Don't take any fruit from that tree—in fact, God says don't even touch it!" I'm taking a few liberties with this passage, but I want to make two points here concerning the first man and first woman.

YOU HAVE TO SPEND TIME WITH GOD
TO HEAR HIS VOICE

First of all, a man should stand in his role and hear from God for his family.

Adam did this. He heard from God personally. He knew first-hand what God said about the trees of the garden.

Every member of the family should seek God's face and commune with Him themselves, but there is a special mantle on a man to lead his family. The only way a man can hear from God is by spending time with God (even if it means turning off the football game to do it).

Frankly, when a woman knows that her husband has heard from God, it is pretty easy for her to follow his lead in most things. Yet she has to hear from God as well so she can *help* her husband in his weak or blind areas (and every man has them in abundance).

Sir, if you are going to be the leader of your home, you must understand that *leadership always carries a burden of responsibility.* There is no such thing as a free ride. That goes for leadership in any area, whether it is in the home, the local church, the community or the nation. Laziness and leadership just don't mix.

COMMUNICATE WITH YOUR FAMILY

Secondly, every husband must communicate with his wife. Communication is the key to healthy, happy relationships and lifelong marriages. The days of "the strong, silent type of man" who cannot or will not talk to his spouse are over.

The only way to fulfill your biblical duties to everybody in your family is to *communicate.* You have to talk to your children and spend time talking with your wife. (Remember that true communication is a two-way street of listening *and* talking, not just talking.)

Adam did well when he heard a sure word from God and then communicated it to his wife, Eve. Things began to go downhill from that point, however.

When Eve told the serpent what her husband had said God said, Satan laid aside his subtle ways and bluntly said:

> **And the serpent said unto the woman, Ye shall not surely die:**
> **For God doth know that in the day ye eat thereof, then your eyes shall be opened, and ye shall be as gods, knowing good and evil.**
> **Genesis 3:4,5**

What would you have done in Eve's situation? If you didn't have the Bible, if you weren't present during the conversation and if your *original source* weren't around, you would be in a difficult position. The problem is that Adam *was* there during the serpent's assault on Eve's faith.

When the serpent challenged God's words, Eve should have pointed that snake directly *to the man who was there*. Adam had the authority and personal assurance of a first-hand witness, so he was equipped to deal with the devil. It is certain that Eve was just as intelligent and valuable as Adam, but in that discussion with Satan she was out of position.

Adam wasn't out picking roots or counting animals while all of this was going on with Eve. Genesis 3:6 tells us Adam was "with her." He was standing there the whole time, just listening to that snake work over his wife with the tongue of doubt and unbelief.

Remember that we are talking about the devilish devices and sin traps that cause people to fall. Satan's tricks have not changed, and this interchange reveals two serious pitfalls that are classic techniques the devil uses against Christians every single day!

One Trap Is Labeled "I Can Handle This by Myself"

First, Eve fell right into the trap of thinking, *I can handle this. I don't need a man.* (Men do the same thing, only they think, *I can handle this. I don't need a* woman's *help.*)

Adam and Eve were placed together for a divine reason. It should be obvious that Adam needed Eve and Eve needed Adam. The same is true for us today. None of us can function perfectly alone. Of course, single people can maintain a home, pursue careers and go through the basic functions of life without the assistance of a mate, but that doesn't mean they were created to live that way forever.

The fact is that the true name of this pitfall is *pride*. Satan started dealing with Eve's pride immediately when he whispered, "You can be like God. You can make your own decisions. You can have your own way. You can do what you want. You can be as God, knowing good and evil."

She began to think, *Yeah! I can do it my way! I know what my husband said that God said. But I can do it my own way.* The problem is that once you begin to think you can do things your way, you begin to pay special attention to the forbidden. Eve looked even closer at the tree and *saw* that it was pretty and pleasant to the eyes, that it was "a tree to be desired to make one wise."

If you pay attention to the forbidden, it will attract you and cause you to do the next thing that Eve did. She touched it. Then she partook of it. Then, as so often happens with sin, she passed it on to somebody else.

Adam Failed To Stand for Truth and Protect His Wife

The second pitfall involves Adam. He passively listened and watched while that cunning serpent essentially called him a liar, set aside the Word of God and questioned the motives of the Almighty! *Adam failed to stand for the truth and protect his wife.*

Every man must protect his wife and family, and anyone else who is under his authority. It is his responsibility under God to protect them at all cost. That is part of what makes a man a man.

My oldest son, Andre, is a successful pastor today, but when he was as young as eight years old, my wife and I began to teach him about his responsibility as a *protector*. Whenever I had to leave the house, I told Andre, "You are responsible for everybody in the house when I am gone. You may only be eight years old, but you are still going to be the man. Do you understand? You are going to protect these ladies while I'm gone. Period. Get used to it."

Andre knew what I expected of him. If I came home and heard that the ladies in my home weren't taken care of, then I wanted to see my eight-year-old son. You start with young ones *early*. Don't wait until a boy is fourteen to suddenly teach him how to be a man. The same goes for teaching young girls how to be strong women of God.

Adam failed when he didn't protect his wife. *Whenever a man does not do his job, catastrophe always comes to the rest of the family.* When the head of a home goes down, everybody else goes down with him, one way or another. Adam didn't take a stand, leaving Satan's lies unchallenged. Since Adam didn't step into his place, the door was opened for the serpent to persuade Eve to step out of hers.

THE SECOND DEVILISH DEVICE: IGNITE A LUST FOR GODHOOD

Satan revealed another devilish device in Genesis 3 when he said: "For God doth know that in the day ye eat thereof, then your eyes shall be opened, and ye shall be as gods, knowing good and evil" (Gen. 3:5).

The serpent was appealing to the lust of "being your own god and calling your own shots." At this point, Eve was still without sin, but her willingness to listen to Satan's lies had put her on the "slippery slope" of temptation. Satan tried the same tactic on Jesus when he offered him "all the kingdoms of the world, and the glory of them" (Matt. 4:8). Jesus didn't listen to Satan's temptations. He always cut him off with the sword of the Spirit—the Word of God.

Many Christians deal with Satan's temptations as Eve did, so it isn't surprising that large numbers of us who show up for church on Sunday mornings live our lives as though we are our own gods.

"Wait a minute, Bishop. The Bible says we are not to have any gods before God our Creator. I don't have any idols!"

No? Any time you decide what you are going to do with your life and how you are going to do it without regard to God's Word and without "seeking first the Kingdom," you have declared your intention to become your own god.

WE ARE TO ACKNOWLEDGE GOD AND FOLLOW HIS LEAD

Does Proverbs 3:6 say, "Acknowledge God in all your ways, and *you* shall decide what path you take?" No, the Scriptures say to acknowledge God and *He* will direct your path.

What is the problem with making a few decisions here and there? The problem is that God's Word says, "There is a way which seemeth right unto a man, but the end thereof are the ways of death" (Prov. 14:12). The big difference between directing things yourself and allowing God to direct you really shows up when things go wrong (and you can count on it some time or another).

If you are on God's path and trouble comes your way, you can go to God's Word and declare, "I am standing on Your Word and obeying Your will, Lord. I am doing what You said, and I am expecting by faith that You will do what Your Word says." Isaiah 43:25 says, "Declare thou, that thou mayest be justified."

You can stand on the Word, and having done all to stand, stand therefore. (See Ephesians 6:13,14.) You will get deliverance in times of trouble *when He directs your path.*

Things aren't so positive when you direct yourself into something and trouble catches up with you. You have nothing to stand on except your own words, and you will go down with the ship.

Let me warn you not to tell yourself, *Well, that was Adam and Eve. I would never fall for that old trick.* Are you that much smarter than Adam and Eve?

ONLY THE NAME HAS BEEN CHANGED

Satan hasn't changed. He is still doing the same things he did in Paradise long ago. In the words of popular police documentaries, "Only the name has been changed," but in this case, it's *to deceive* the innocent. The latest name tag for the world's oldest lie is "humanism," the feel-good, be-your-own-god heresy that has successfully infiltrated America's educational system under the guise of a "philosophy." The lie is still the same, and so are its consequences.

DON'T LISTEN TO THINGS CONTRARY
TO THE WORD OF GOD

The Bible says, "The woman saw that the tree was good for food, and that it was pleasant to the eyes..." (Gen. 3:6). Eve fell into sin *after* she listened to what the enemy said and failed to reject it. You cannot afford to listen to things contrary to the Word of God. Stop the conversation and say, "I've got to go," or, "You've got to be quiet." If you are going to listen, then eventually you may acquire a serious *sight problem*.

The longer you listen to Satan's lies, the more likely it is that something he says will capture your imagination. In Eve's case, she *saw* that the tree was good for food and that it was pleasant to the eyes.

I don't consider myself to be a great authority on the subject, but in my years of ministry and marriage, I've noticed that women tend to like beautiful things. Most men will walk right by a beautiful bouquet of flowers without a second thought because they are thinking about other things like food, a challenge they are facing or a woman. A woman will stop to look at that bouquet and smell its delicate fragrances. She will invest time and effort to display that bouquet in just the right vase and position it to catch just the right light. Then her female friends will come over and immediately tell her, "That is so pretty!" There is nothing wrong with the female appreciation of beauty—God made women that way (and men should thank Him for it regularly).

Men tend to have a different kind of sight problem. I may be exaggerating, but I think nearly 98 percent of the male sight problem revolves around the beauty that walks by on two shapely female legs and possesses the power to capture *all* of his attention in the blink (or wink) of an eye.

SIGHT PROBLEMS WILL GET YOU IN TROUBLE

Whether you are male or female, sight problems will get you in trouble. Jesus warned us in the gospel of Matthew to keep our eyes from evil. (See Matthew 6:22,23.) In other words, let your eyes look right on (and that is doubly true for men).

Jesus said a man has sinned if he commits adultery in his heart by looking at a woman long enough to lust for her. (See Matthew 5:28.) Jesus emphasized the "looking" part for a reason: Men are very visual.

A man will always notice when a good-looking woman passes by—even if his wife is sitting right next to him. The "noticing" goes beyond morality or holiness; God made the male that way. Every wife knows this. After all, how did she capture her husband's attention in the first place? The problem isn't in the noticing; it's in the *looking*.

A godly man will notice a beautiful woman, realize she is another wonder in God's creation and *turn away* with his eyes, his mind and his heart without sin. The Bible says we should deal with lust by running away from it, not by "rebuking, confessing and fasting" over it. Those things are valuable tools for other battles, but the battle over sight problems is won by turning away.

IT'S THE LOOKING THAT DOES THE HOOKING

Trouble always comes when we keep on "looking," whether the looker is a male or a female.

Women *are* a little different from men in the area of sexual temptation. They are more susceptible to wooing words and a gentle touch than to exposed flesh.

A beautiful woman can meet a man who is uglier than the south end of an elephant, but she may fall in love with him if he talks to her nicely and takes time to listen to her. Her heart will melt if he will value, assist and understand her. She will take him to her heart and overlook his appearance because of the way he relates to her.

Eve's sight problem shows up in verse 6 of the Garden temptation passage: "And when the woman *saw* that the tree was good for food, and that it was *pleasant to the eyes,* and a tree *to be desired to make one wise, she took* of the fruit thereof" (Gen. 3:6).

EVE LOOKED HARD AND FORGOT HER MAN AND HER GOD

Satan *captivated,* or enslaved, Eve with the snare of pride and the lust of the eye. The more Eve listened to the serpent and gazed at the forbidden tree, the more she forgot about her man and her God.

Don't allow yourself to be mesmerized by the "pretty" and desirable things that the world offers, because sin is almost always attached to them somehow. Remember that Romans 6:23 says, "The wages of sin is death." That "tree" you are looking at may look good and it may smell good, but there's death in its fruit. It might walk on two legs and talk a good talk, but if it is sin, it will still end with death.

Eve lost her relationship and fellowship with God and she almost lost her husband too. Why? Her sight problem caused her to forget about everything but her desires. Don't be moved by the things that you see. Instead, be moved by the God in whom you believe.

"WORD PEOPLE" ARE HEAVENLY ASSAULT WEAPONS

Satan challenges God's Word because he knows what we seem to forget so easily: If he does not challenge the Word of God in your life, then you will become a Word man or a Word woman. That means you become dangerous to his dark kingdom. You literally become heaven's assault weapon to the kingdom of hell. When you go by what you see instead of what you know by God's Word, you are in danger.

God warned Adam, "for in the day that thou eatest thereof thou shalt surely die" (Gen. 2:17). God wasn't saying Adam and Eve would fall over dead the second they took a bite of forbidden fruit; He was warning them they would die spiritually by being separated from Him. This is the most heinous kind of death for eternal creatures designed for continuous fellowship with divinity.

121

Despite God's direct warning, Adam made the mistake that countless men and women still make today.

Eve partook of the forbidden fruit first, and instantly she died spiritually. I believe you could see a difference in her the moment God's glory left her.

The man was still in the glory at that point because he hadn't partaken of the forbidden fruit. Now he faced a choice: He could obey God and keep God number one in his life, or he could choose the woman.

Adam looked at that woman and heard her say in her most persuasive tone, "Come on Adam, take it with me." He continued to *look* at that woman while he thought about what God said. Then he looked at that good-looking woman again and thought about what God said yet another time: "This means death."

ADAM CHOSE DEATH WITH EVE OVER LIFE WITH GOD

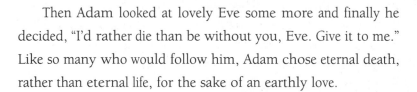

Then Adam looked at lovely Eve some more and finally he decided, "I'd rather die than be without you, Eve. Give it to me." Like so many who would follow him, Adam chose eternal death, rather than eternal life, for the sake of an earthly love.

Satan's nature came up in the first man and woman immediately because they sinned, and the very nature of death flooded their being. Now they had the very nature of the devil and were separated from God by their uncovered sin. (Thank God that He is longsuffering toward us. Aren't you glad that God doesn't just throw us away when we mess up and act ignorantly?)

My friend, no one born on the face of this earth is worth the cost of turning away from God and losing your salvation. Men and women will disappoint you, but God never will.

EVE WAS DECEIVED, BUT ADAM *CHOSE* HIS FATE

Timothy tells us that Eve was deceived, while Adam was not. Unlike Eve, Adam understood precisely what was happening. He understood what the serpent was saying, and he knew what his wife was doing. He fully understood the ramifications of Eve's actions and of what was going on in his own mind.

Adam made a clear-cut, conscious decision to defy God's command, and according to the apostle Paul, the result was that "in Adam *all* die" (1 Cor. 15:22). God would hold Adam particularly responsible for his decision and actions, and He still holds men particularly responsible as protectors and leaders to this day.

Adam and Eve were already dead spiritually when *the voice of God* "came walking in the garden in the cool of the day" (Gen. 3:7). They realized they were naked, and mankind experienced shame for the first time since Creation. When they heard God's voice moving closer and closer, they hid themselves in shame and fear.

It was in that moment that Eve discovered "the knowledge of good and evil" wasn't all it was cracked up to be. It was a fearful thing to know that they had sinned and that their sinless Creator was coming closer.

PARADISE WAS OMINOUSLY QUIET

When God called out for Adam, Paradise was ominously quiet. "Adam." No answer. "Adam. Come out, Boy" (this is the way the dramatized Butler translation reads). Finally God said something like, "What is your problem?" and Adam finally answered.

> And he said, I heard thy voice in the garden, and I was afraid, because I was naked; and I hid myself.
> And he said, Who told thee that thou wast naked? Hast thou eaten of the tree, whereof I commanded thee that thou shouldest not eat?
> And the man said, The woman whom thou gavest to be with me, she gave me of the tree, and I did eat.
>
> Genesis 3:10-12

Adam did what men still do today when he said, "She did it. It was that woman *You* gave me!" He refused to take responsibility for his own actions, and then he even tried to blamed God for it (as though Adam didn't want Eve! Pardon me, but didn't Adam just choose Eve over God and eternal life in Paradise?).

Eve didn't do much better:

> And the Lord God said unto the woman, What is this that thou hast done? And the woman said, The serpent beguiled me, and I did eat.
>
> Genesis 3:13

MEN AND WOMEN ARE EQUALLY QUICK TO PASS OFF GUILT

There is no room for gender-based pride in this situation: Where sin is concerned, there is *no difference* between men and

124

women. Both are equally quick to pass off their guilt on others. This too, is a favorite tactic the enemy uses against believers.

God is always interested in honest confession, repentance and complete forgiveness; but Satan only wants us to point the finger in endless blame games that combine guilt and shame with the sins of being a false witness and judging one another.

Once God heard what Adam and Eve had to say, He dealt with each party to the sin one by one. In Genesis 3:15, God began His judgment with the father of lies and spoke prophetically that Satan's head would be bruised by Eve's seed (God's seed in Jesus Christ). He told the devil what was coming, but since Satan has been stripped of his anointing, he has also been stripped of his ability to receive *revelation*. He heard what God said, but didn't have the revelation to fully understand the plans of God.

Secondly, God dealt with Eve and told her that her relationship to her husband was fundamentally changed by her sin. It is sin that stripped Eve of her equality with Adam. Praise God, Jesus came to redeem womankind from the curse of the fall. After Calvary, the original order and plan of God remains, but not the pain of the Garden failure that lowered Eve's status.

Woman was deceived, but man made a wrong decision knowingly. Eve's error took womankind down a step in the social order and in physical safety and comfort until Jesus restored her to her original position. Adam's sin took *all mankind*—male and female—straight to the grave. Once again, it took the Son of God Himself to bring us to a glorious resurrection.

Now we have examined Satan's devices of deception, and we are forewarned and forearmed. Divine knowledge revealed in the

Bible is God's solution for human ignorance and devilish deception. The Lord has given us everything we need to succeed; now
the rest is up to us.

God's Plan for Marriage:
It's Leave and Cleave, Not Cleave and Leave

Divorce is one of the greatest indictments against the Church of Jesus Christ in our generation. You would think that with all of God's promises and heaven's resources at our disposal, the Church would manage to do better than "match" the world's divorce rate.

The problem is all too familiar: We failed to follow God's plan for man in marriage. It is clearly spelled out in the Bible: "Therefore shall a man *leave* his father and his mother, and shall *cleave* unto his wife: and they shall be one flesh" (Gen. 2:24).

Marriage partners who "leave and cleave" will tend to succeed; while those who don't, won't.

The Bible says a man is supposed to *leave* his father and mother. You don't need any Hebrew word meanings for this one. If Mama is still trying to hold onto a man with her apron strings, he has to cut them before he marries a woman.

A wise bride leaves that task to her husband. No matter what she thinks about her new mother-in-law, she should respect her to the best of her ability. It is up to the husband to say, "Mama, I love you, but this isn't your house, this isn't your kitchen, and this isn't your place of authority."

A man also must leave the control and authority of his father in order to establish his own life. Of course, he should always respect and honor his parents, but that doesn't mean they are to *control* him once he leaves home to set up his own house.

GOD'S PLAN: "CLING, ADHERE, HOLD TIGHT, PURSUE HARD"

The Hebrew word translated "cleave" means "to cling or adhere, to catch by pursuit, to stick to, follow close, be joined, keep (tightly), pursue hard."[1] It doesn't get much clearer than this.

When the Bible says a man will leave father and mother, it means he will *leave* to get out on his own. He will get his own place and learn how to take care of himself. He needs to learn how to handle money before he marries, because it takes money and sound money management to maintain a house and home for two.

In a sense, the Lord isn't referring to a man's leaving mother and father only. He is really talking about the man's entire family and closest circle of friendships. The point is that when a man marries, his wife has to take first place above everyone else but God. That includes a man's "buddies" too.

Every so often I'll play ball with some of my male friends, but I don't run with "the guys" three and four days a week to play football, baseball or hang out at the bowling alley or gym.

If you're going to have a wife, then that means that she has to be first to the exclusion of all others. She gets first rights on your time, energy and money. Everybody else has to line up after that. She is number one.

SINGLE MEN HAVEN'T FOUND THEIR "GOOD THING" YET

Married men have no business carrying on and running around as though they are still single, and they shouldn't be running around with single men either. Single men can stay out all night and do whatever they want to do within the bounds of the law. That is because they have not yet found their "good thing" from the Lord. (See Proverbs 18:22.)

Married women should not run with single women either. A single woman doesn't have to report to anyone in most cases, and she can spend her money on whatever she wants and go wherever she feels like going. If you are married, you can't and you shouldn't do these things.

You certainly should never let some single woman tell you what she would do if she were you. She's not you. She doesn't have your man, and she is not in your situation. When she marries a husband, you can be sure she is going to change her tune. Things change when you enter an intimate life partnership.

God has a plan; and if we follow God's plan, we can avoid the messes and enjoy the blessings. Things break down and go bad quickly when we follow our own plans and do things our own way.

NEVER BYPASS THE WISDOM OF GOD'S WORD

The worst thing we can do is bypass God's Word and follow the lead of our feelings or the unbiblical "counsel" of our hairstylist, our favorite TV star or even Mama and, in some cases, Daddy.

Even a bride has to leave her family when she walks down the aisle to marry her husband. She has to be willing to cut Mama's apron strings if she wants her marriage to last. Most godly parents know this and do everything they can to make the transition a healthy experience, but some parents lose focus and become reluctant to "let go" of their grown children.

If you are single and you are not ready to let your mama go, then you are not ready to get married. I don't care what your body tells you, or what Auntie May or Cousin Mimi says.

If you are already married but you always spend all of your time at Mama's house, or if you talk on the phone to her constantly, then something's wrong. I am not saying you should stop loving your mama and cut off all communication with her. No, I am talking about a compulsive relationship that makes you think you can't survive without your mother's direct input in your life every single day. Counselors call this a "codependent" relationship.

Something is wrong if you tell your husband, "I can't move out of town because all my family is here." It may be difficult, but you and your husband have become a new creation. You are two made into one. If your husband goes to Timbuktu, then you had better get to Timbuktu too. Where he goes, you go.

HE IS HIGHER THAN YOUR DADDY!

Some might protest, "Well, he isn't my daddy!" I have to agree. He *isn't* your daddy. *He is higher than your daddy—he is your husband.* Daddy becomes the number-two man in your life the moment you say, "I do."

It hurts me to admit this fact because the day will come all too quickly when I will have to give away my own daughters in marriage. On that day I am going to be relegated to the number-two position in their lives too. It hurts, but it is the way of life and it is the only way to help my daughters build strong marriages that will stand the test of time.

Many young brides make the mistake of running to their mamas to tell them every unpleasant thing that happens in their new marriages. They rarely stop there. Once the pity train is going, they just naturally want to tell their sisters, brothers, cousins, girlfriends, old boyfriends and daddies.

In the short term, these young brides may feel better. The downside is that even though they may go back home and make up with their new husbands that same night, their families never absorb the good news of reconciliation.

Everything may be fine with the newlyweds the morning after, but the bride's family members will be thinking, *If that jerk steps out of line one more time, I'm going to get my gun! Then I'll just repent after I kill him!*

Mature Women, Teach The Young Brides

God knows it isn't easy for young wives to live with their difficult husbands, so He has a plan for this situation too. Speaking through the apostle Paul's letter to Titus his disciple, God says in His Word:

> **But speak thou the things which become sound doctrine:**
>
> [To] **the aged women likewise, that they be in behaviour as becometh holiness, not false accusers, not given to much wine, teachers of good things;**
>
> *That they may teach the young women to...love their husbands.*
>
> **Titus 2:1,3,4**

Very few Christian couples, or churches for that matter, observe this biblical command. It is obvious. Frustrated and desperate young brides cry through entire church services while mature women, deep wells of marital wisdom, sit nearby unaware of their pain. It is time to tap the resources God gave to us in His wisdom.

If you do things God's way you will enjoy divine blessings; if you do things man's way, you reap more of what you sowed— man's foolishness. God wants the more mature wives in His body to counsel young brides in the fine art of loving their husbands and building a home that will be a beacon of hope.

God knows what He's talking about. He gave us the divine formula for happy, lifelong marriage relationships when He commanded us to "leave and cleave."

If you're not ready to leave and cleave, then you are not ready for marriage. If you are already married and are doing the wrong thing, correct it right now. Get in line with God's Word so things will begin to work better for you.

DON'T LET THE DATING STOP WHEN THE RINGS GO ON

When God's Word says, "Therefore shall a man leave his father and his mother, and shall cleave unto his wife" in Genesis 2:24, every husband should take it as his cue to run after his bride and date her for life. It is his divine commission to stay close to her—very close.

I understand that many men just don't know how to treat their wives, and they don't seem to understand the need to show them affection after the honeymoon is over. That is why I'm teaching these things.

Before the "I do's," that young man dated his true love with determination and endless energy. He was hanging around her house every spare moment of the day or night. He was in her parent's house so much they were tired of seeing his face.

That young lady couldn't go anywhere without seeing that boy's face all the time. Every time she turned a corner, there he was with that stupid-looking grin on his face.

Ladies are the same way. Before the wedding, you just couldn't seem to snuggle close enough to that man. If you were sitting in a car that didn't have bucket seats, your place was right there next to him, glued to the side of his body. He even had to avoid right turns because you had his arm in a love lock.

AFTER THE HONEYMOON, HIS HUMANITY STARTS SHOWING

After the honeymoon is over and the realities of his humanity become clear to you, he doesn't have any problems making right turns anymore. For some reason, there is now a vast chilly space separating the two of you in the front of the car. In fact, he has to warn you about left turns because you are glued to the passenger door and about to fall out of the window.

It doesn't have to be that way. "Well, we are married now, so it's different." No, it doesn't have to be different. You can still be close and excited about one another even after twenty, forty or sixty years of marriage. *Cleave unto each other.* That is part of God's plan for man.

Let me clarify what should be obvious: God said, "Therefore shall a man leave his father and mother," *not* "Therefore shall a man *leave his wife.*"

WELCOME TO THE GROWING IRRECONCILABLE MINORITY

The world has created a new business profit center and a large new demographic class of people by mass-producing divorces based on so-called "irreconcilable differences." All that means is that two people claim they can't get along. It seems like these divorced "irreconcilables" comprise one of the fastest growing segments of the American population.

Two people who are filled with the Holy Ghost and enter a church service carrying Bibles in their hands to sing, "We lift our hands, and we offer You the sacrifice of praise..." have no business going home and shouting at each other, "Shut up! I can't stand you!" There is something wrong with this picture.

What are people talking about when they say they have irreconcilable differences? It means they want to get divorced because they can't get along. How can Christians talk like this and still call themselves "saved, sanctified, full-of-the- Holy-Ghost-with-a-mighty-burning-fire Christians"?

God's opinion of divorce is consistent throughout the Old and New Testaments. He hates it. The last Old Testament prophet, Malachi, had something chilling to say to "religious" people—men in particular—who wanted divorces.

> **And this is the second thing you do: You cover the altar of the Lord with tears, with weeping and crying;** *so He does not regard the offering anymore,* **nor receive it with goodwill from your hands.**
> **Yet you say, "For what reason?" Because the Lord has been witness between you and** *the wife of your youth, with whom you have dealt treacherously;* **yet she is your companion and your wife by covenant.**
> **Malachi 2:13,14** NKJV

The prophet was uncovering the hypocrisy of "religious" men who squalled and bawled at God's altar and offered Him lavish gifts, and then wondered why He wouldn't accept their sacrifices.

The reason was simple: God refused to accept their sacrifice because these men were dumping the wives they married in their youth once they reached their prime (probably their forties). Then they wanted to marry some young thing and ask God's blessing on their lives. It doesn't work that way.

I married young and now that I am forty-plus, my wife and I have already celebrated more than twenty years together as husband and wife.

AT LAST, I FINALLY KNOW SOMETHING

By the time a man reaches middle age, he finally knows something about life, marriage and his vocation. It is during these years that men tend to reach the peak of their earning potential and enjoy a measure of financial security.

Middle-aged men are old enough now to really know what they are doing, and they are still young enough to do it. That is the reason we see so many twenty-five-year-old young ladies trying to grab forty-year-old men as husbands. These men have all of the trappings of prosperity and security. They don't have to build their careers—they are already at the top floor of their businesses, vocations and callings.

Today men are guilty of doing the same thing the Israelite husbands in Malachi's day were doing. They marry young, and expect their wives to loyally stand by them while they struggle to earn college degrees, build their businesses, establish their careers or ministries and start a family. After the years of struggle are over, these men want to jettison the "wives of their youth" so they can marry much younger women and enjoy their hard-earned rewards with them instead of with the women who paid the price for their success.

YOU HAVE DEALT TREACHEROUSLY

Then these "cleavers and leavers" would waltz into the temple and offer sactimonious sacrifices to God as though He was supposed to be impressed by their offerings. How soon we forget that God sees and knows all things. His response to these men is still His response today: The Lord has been witness between you and the wife of your youth, with whom you have dealt treacherously" (Mal. 2:14 NKJV).

Then the Lord goes on to explain why He hates divorce so much:

> **But did He not make them one, having a remnant of the Spirit? And why one?** *He seeks godly offspring.* **Therefore take heed to your spirit, And let none deal treacherously with the wife of his youth.**
>
> **"For the Lord God of Israel says that He hates divorce, for it covers one's garment with violence," says the Lord of hosts.**
>
> **Malachi 2:15,16 NKJV**

God wants us to marry born-again believers *because He seeks godly seed.* It is no accident that my children are called to the ministry. There is such a thing as a "generational anointing" that is a crucial component of God's plan for man.

THE TRUE PURPOSE OF GENERATIONAL ANOINTING: GODLY SEED

Everyone knows that tendencies toward alcholism, drug abuse and witchcraft tend to be passed down from parents to children for generations (barring supernatural intervention by the power of God). This is but a dim picture of the true purpose of generational transference—God wants to pass on the anointing

He placed on you and your spouse to your children, only in greater measure!

God wants godly seed. If you are godly and your spouse is godly, then your children should turn out to be godly as well. If they don't, there is something seriously wrong.

ABORTION IS JUST A DEVICE OF THE ENEMY TO STEAL SEED

You probably already know that abortion is another way the enemy tries to steal God's seed from the earth. When a male and a female human put their dust together, they create more dust that looks like them. But it is God who puts life in that little body. We can create bodies through the reproduction process, but God puts His own life in the body because He seeks godly seed.

"Yeah, but I have a right to do what I want with my own body."

Yes, you have a right to do what you want with *your* own body, but we aren't talking about *your* body. We are talking about the body of somebody else who is inside of your body.

Your body is just an incubator that keeps that new human being warm and fed. God put the breath of life inside that little person; it is a living soul, and it is God's seed.

God's final warning to the "leavers and cleavers" may not be politically correct, but that doesn't matter. This is God talking:

> **Therefore take heed to your spirit, And let none deal treacherously with the wife of his youth.**

**"For the Lord God of Israel says that He hates divorce,
for it covers one's garment with violence.**

Malachi 2:15,16

God hates divorce. Now, if you have already gone through a divorce from your spouse, I must tell you that divorce is not the unpardonable sin. There is still mercy and grace to cover all of our mistakes, misjudgments and failures.

EVERY KEY YOU NEED TO SUCCEED IN MARRIAGE!

God's plan for man, and His plan for preserving Christian marriage relationships in particular, is summed up in a single chapter of the Bible. The thirteenth chapter of Paul's first epistle to the Corinthians contains every key we need to succeed in our marriages.

Paul declared by the Spirit, "Charity [or love] never faileth (1 Cor. 13:8). He was talking about *agape* love, the "God-kind-of-love" which is "shed abroad in our hearts by the Holy Ghost" according to Romans 5:5.

Love never fails. What does the word "never" mean? It means it will not fail "at any time." Love always works because it never fails. That makes it difficult for Christians to "reconcile" themselves with the concept of divorce for the sake of "irreconcilable differences." God designed marriage to be a lifelong covenant that is not to be broken by man or woman.

The Word declares that "charity [love] suffereth long" (1 Cor. 13:4). Real love isn't some kind of slurpy, syrupy concoction that loses its power after the first taste or two. The love that anchors marriages for a lifetime goes way beyond the temporary psychological and biochemical thrill we call "falling in love."

OUR BODIES MAY FADE BUT REAL LOVE GETS STRONGER

Real love doesn't fade just because wrinkles begin to gather around the face and middle-age fat deposits begin to gather around the waist. It lasts, and thank God for it. The ravages of aging will ultimately come to everyone, from your grandmother to the beauty queens and handsome movie stars we see on the silver screen.

The Bible says that the outward man perishes, but the inward man is renewed day by day. (See 2 Corinthians 4:16.) True love springs from that "inner man or woman."

If your love for your spouse is based on how nice they look, then your love and your marriage is going to fade away quickly. If it is based primarily on other outward characteristics, you are also in trouble. "I like how she speaks...I like the way he talks...I'm in love."

Someone once said, "Love is blind, *but marriage is an eye-opener.*" I'll second that opinion. You can count on one thing in marriage: Things are going to change between the time you are dating and the time you leave the altar. After you get married, you will see another side of your spouse that you never knew existed!

I heard a story about a traveling evangelist who needed some help with music in his ministry. He met a woman who could sing like a mockingbird and he thought, *"Man, she would be a great asset to my ministry."* So he married her thinking about the great asset she would be to his ministry.

After the wedding night, he woke up in the morning and looked at her. She had no make-up on her face and to his surprise, her hair was sitting on the desk. All he knew to do was look away and say, "Woman, sing! Sing!"

You will find out whether you have real love or not when the dishes are piled up as high as your shoulder, or when little ones come along with diapers that are oozing goo. Real love will show up when you've been working for twenty-five consecutive days to pay a medical bill.

IS IT LOVE, OR LUST DRESSED UP AS LOVE?

Marriage will prove whether you have real love for one another, or simply met at the altar based on lust dressed up as love.

The apostle Paul really starts to "mess with things" in the next verse when he writes:

> **[Charity] is kind; charity envieth not; charity vaunteth not itself, is not puffed up,**
> **Doth not behave itself unseemly, seeketh not her own, is not easily provoked, thinketh no evil....**
> **1 Corinthians 13:4,5**

Envy and "puffed-up pride" have fractured the foundations of countless marriages over the centuries. When Paul warns us about behaving in an unseemly manner, he is saying, "Don't be rude." Rudeness creates unbearable friction in the close quarters of a marriage relationship. It is never acceptable, but especially when it is directed toward a spouse.

When Paul says love "seeketh not her own," *The Amplified Bible* says it means love "seeks not her own way." If you think you always have to have your own way in your marriage, then you aren't extending love toward your spouse, you're entangling your mate with control.

LOSE THE INVENTORY OF PAST WRONGS

Paul says love isn't easily provoked and that it "thinketh no evil." That means that if you really love someone, you will always think the best about that person, no matter what slander and gossip you hear. It also means you won't keep any record or inventory of past wrongs.

People who go into a marriage relationship with a poor self-image often think the worst about their spouse because they feel so badly about themselves and have such low self-confidence. They keep a running total of everything their spouse ever did to offend, anger or hurt them. Worst of all, they are always ready to "replay" their "They Done Me Wrong" video at the slightest signal.

Anytime something seems to go wrong, insecure spouses will begin to question themselves and their spouses as well. Their constant suspicions can even begin to weaken the foundations of their marriage.

If your spouse arrives home twenty minutes late because the car had to be freed from a snow drift in the parking lot, do you meet your victim at the front door and start the arrest routine: "Where have you been?! You were supposed to have been here twenty minutes ago! Are you seeing somebody?! I'll *kill* the fool!"

ANGRY TIRADES AND STEAMED WINDOWS

I even see it at the church occasionally. At times I've seen some poor husband getting an earful from his angry wife, and the tirade will continue for a quarter of an hour before they manage to leave the parking lot. The windows steam up, people a block away are staring; but only a half hour before, the couple had been standing side-by-side singing, "Oh, how I love Jesus...."

Paul goes on to say, "[Love] rejoiceth not in iniquity, but rejoiceth in the truth; Beareth all things..." (1 Cor. 13:5). The first part is easy enough to understand, but what is Paul saying about "bearing all things?" What does that mean? It means that love "covers all things with silence, it endures and suffers patiently."[2]

Not only that, but love also "believeth all things, hopeth all things, endureth all things" (1 Cor. 13:7).

It is in the next verse that Paul writes, "Charity (love) never fails." Let me say something that may shock you if you aren't married, but it is nonetheless true: You don't really fall in love with someone until *after* you've been married to them.

All the other feel-good things that happen in courtship aren't real love. These things aren't necessarily bad, and anyone has to admit they feel awfully good, but they aren't real love.

143

You don't "fall" into real love; *you grow love.* You grow it over time until you come to a place that when your mate inhales, you exhale: You both share the same breath.

Therefore shall a man *leave* his father and his mother, and shall *cleave* unto his wife: and they shall be one flesh.

Genesis 2:24

This is God's divine plan for mankind and for marriage. Any time you tinker with God's plan, somebody pays a terrible price. For the last twenty-five years pop-psychology and experimental psychiatry have tinkered with America's ideas about sex, marriage and divorce. Where divorce is concerned, our children have been stuck with the painful bill for our foolishness.

THE DAMAGE OF DIVORCE IS WORSE THAN WE THOUGHT...

The psychologists lied to you twenty-five years ago when they said children don't really suffer when their parents divorce. Now they turn around and say, "After twenty years of analyzing actual case studies of broken homes, we found out that the damage to the kids is worse than we thought. Now we say it is better that parents stay together for the sake of the children."

It doesn't do much good for social tinkerers to come back twenty years later and say, "Oh, we made a mistake." The damage is done. They didn't know what they were talking about, but the world was listening anyway.

It's always better to have two, a man and woman, who will get in God's Word and work it out in love and just keep working on it. At least then the child will see that you don't just cut and run because things get tough. If they see you run from difficulty then they are going to cut and run in school, on the job, in their relationships and in everything else they try.

LEARN TO STAND!

Believe God and stand on His Word; then you will get God's power involved in your situation. When God's power gets involved, your situation may still *look* hopeless; but; remember, there is no hopelessness with God! He is Hope! He is Life! He is Love itself, and He is the One who can set your marriage back on a firm foundation that will stand the test of time and adversity.

The only way this happens is if you give God a chance to restore what has been lost, broken or stolen from you. That will never happen if you cut and run from your problems and so-called "irreconcilable differences"! Love *never* fails. It is time to do things God's way. It is time to leave and *cleave for life.*

God's Plan for the Flesh
(And Satan's Haunting Wish)

Did you ever notice that when people die and leave their bodies, they don't have any authority on the earth anymore? They don't *stop existing;* they simply give up their temporary "lease" on their earthly residence and move "out of the mortal state."

Throughout this chapter, you should remind yourself often that you are not a "body." You are an eternal spirit who possesses a soul and lives in an earthly body for a brief season we call a "human life."

You are "in" a body as you read these words, but the truth is that you will still exist even after you leave your body. You, and every other human being, will go to one of two places after your body dies: You will either go to heaven to be with God, or you will go to hell to spend a tormented eternity with Satan and his fallen angels in the lake of fire.

Regardless of our eternal destination, we will all be alive after death. In fact, every single human being that has ever existed on this planet, beginning with Adam, *is still existing* at this moment in time.

Those who have already departed their earthly bodies are either experiencing eternal life right now, or they are suffering eternal death this very moment. Very few people preach about hell these days; because it isn't considered "PC," "politically correct." My only criteria is whether or not it is "BC," "biblically correct."

Last time I checked, hell was still in the Bible, so I preach a message entitled *"Hell: You Don't Want To Go There."* Basically I say, "There isn't anything down there for you. What in hell do you want? There isn't anything in hell that you want; everything you want is in heaven."

WE ARE AMPHIBIOUS: AT HOME IN BOTH FLESH AND SPIRIT

Why am I emphasizing the body so much? We have already learned that God basically appointed Adam as the "god of this world" under His authority. The reason the enemy came at Adam and Eve was that they were created eternal spirits operating through *physical bodies.* They were "equipped" by God to interact and function in the created realm of matter as well as in the spirit realm, much as amphibious creatures are equally at home on land and in water.

Why is a body so important? The body is a *badge of authority* in the earth. The way to have the greatest range of authority in the earth for good or for evil is to operate through a physical body. That is the reason everyone in the spirit realm wants to "get in you."

God wants to dwell with you in your body by the Holy Ghost, but He will only come in by personal invitation.

Satan wants to dwell inside your body too, but for a totally different reason and under totally different circumstances. It is his haunting wish to *possess* your body, whether he is invited or not.

There are all kinds of possessed people in the world. When you go to church this weekend, the building will be full of "possessed people." In fact, I confess to you that I am possessed (I know you're thinking, *I knew he was!*) I am possessed by the Holy Ghost! I have the God of the universe living on the inside!

JESUS CAME IN THE FLESH

The role of the flesh (the body) in the earthly workings of the spirit realm is of critical importance. It is so important that the apostle John made the confession that Jesus "came in the *flesh*" the primary criterion for judging between clean and unclean spirits:

> **Hereby know ye the Spirit of God: Every spirit that confesseth that *Jesus Christ is come in the flesh* is of God:**
> **And every spirit that confesseth not that Jesus Christ *is come in the flesh* is not of God: and this is that spirit of antichrist, whereof ye have heard that it should come; and even now already is it in the world.**
> **Ye are of God, little children, and have overcome them: *because greater is he that is in you,* than he that is in the world.**
>
> **1 John 4:2-4**

Notice that in the same passage in which John tells us how to discern between clean and unclean spirits operating through human hosts, he notes that the God who "is in you" is greater than the enemy who is in the world.

John was addressing the problem of false prophets and teachers who would try to infiltrate the flock of God while passing themselves off as wise teachers. These men had given their bodies over to evil spirits and were doing the work of Satan under the guise of Christian leadership. John's spiritual "litmus test" quickly set apart the wolves from the sheep.

GOD'S GENESIS ASSIGNMENT FOR THE FLESH HASN'T CHANGED

Despite all of the problems we have with our "flesh" and its appetite for excess, God has a plan for our flesh. He created it, and He knows what it was *really* made for. The core purpose of the human body was spelled out in the book of Genesis when God gave Adam his assignment in the Garden of Eden. The assignment hasn't changed; it simply became clearer because of the finished work of Jesus Christ, the "last Adam." (See 1 Corinthians 15:45-47.)

Jesus' humble invasion of the earth in human flesh was birthed in the heart of God long before Adam was ever created. It happened because God is a very legal Being. When God says something, He fulfills it exactly to the letter. When He sets a boundary or decrees a law, He observes and follows that boundary perfectly.

Did you ever wonder why God didn't just tell the devil in the serpent's body, "Shut up, Devil! I'm just going to start all over again"? God didn't do that because He knew that by His own laws and conditions, He didn't have the authority to do that.

No man, angel or devil could have stopped Him, but He chose to limit Himself according to His own words. No one is big enough to control, stop or influence God. Jesus said, "Heaven and earth shall pass away, but my words shall not pass away" (Matt. 24:35), and He meant it. These words also apply to God's words before Jesus came to the earth, as we see in Isaiah 55:

> **So shall my word be that goeth forth out of my mouth: it shall not return unto me void, but it shall accomplish that which I please, and it shall prosper in the thing whereto I sent it.**
>
> **Isaiah 55:11**

God *always* does what He says. He refuses to violate His own Word or man's free will. That is the divine integrity that placed our Creator in a seemingly impossible position.

He had delegated the authority of ruler and sovereign to man, the only creature made in His own image and after His likeness. As long as the course of man's "lease on earth" continued to run, mankind was caretaker of God's delegated authority over the earth and everything in the earth.

Then came the sin in the Garden of Eden, and Adam and Eve and all of their descendants took on the very nature of the devil after they chose disobedience over eternal relationship with God. Basically, their sinful choice to taste the forbidden fruit made Satan their head, or god, instead of God the Creator.

ADAM AND EVE DIDN'T KNOW SATAN WAS A KILLER

They didn't know what God knew. Satan would be the one who would kill, steal and destroy the descendants of Adam and Eve—but they would soon find out, when murder came to their house.

From man's sin and from the arch-prince of rebellion flowed the chaos and disorder that would disrupt the patterns of the earth, of nature and of human behavior. From these you can trace the hurricanes, floods, famines, wars and atrocities that have plagued man since the Fall.

Jesus drew the line of demarcation in John 10:10 when He said, "The thief cometh not, but for to steal, and to kill, and to destroy: I am come that they might have life, and that they might have it more abundantly."

Paul the apostle told the Corinthian believers that Satan is "the god of this world." (2 Cor. 4:4), but the devil is not god of the believer. Let me repeat that for emphasis: Satan may be the god of this world, but he is *not* god of the believer.

As blood-washed followers of Jesus Christ, our citizenship is in heaven although we live in this world. As citizens of heaven, our bodies have been set apart for holy service.

WE ARE RESIDENT REPRESENTATIVES IN A FOREIGN REALM

The Bible says that we are members of the Kingdom of heaven and ambassadors for Christ. (See Colossians 1:13,

2 Corinthians 5:20.) An ambassador is a "resident representative" of his or her government nation in a foreign land.

You are an ambassador, a representative of your King, residing in a foreign realm. The governing authorities and residents of that realm have no dominion over you as the King's legal ambassador—including the devil and his demons.

Jesus Christ, the Redeemer, came in the flesh because God was determined to redeem His creation *legally*. He had a divine plan for man, and He would not allow man's sin or Satan's hindrances to stop His plan.

God said, "I am not going to let My people, those I created in My own image and after My likeness, stay in their sin. I'm not going to leave them to die for eternity. I refuse to abandon them under Satan's boots to suffer under his cruel heel in slavery. I will give them eternal life. I will put My Word into the earth!"

He had to send a redeemer with the legal right to redeem the race of man from the slavery of sin. They would have to be *purchased* back from Satan's dominion ("redemption" means "to be bought with a price").

THE FATHER OF LIES IS STILL WEAVING HIS WEBS

Man fell into bondage under Satan due to the serpent's trickery. The deceiver stole Adam's headship over the earth with his subtle lies, and the father of lies is still weaving his webs to capture the hearts of people today. Those who are involved in devil worship and the New Age movement are being deceived. He may promise them power but, as always, he is lying.

In the gospel of John, Jesus contrasted God's way with
Satan's way:

> **Verily, verily, I say unto you, He that entereth *not by***
> ***the door* into the sheepfold, but climbeth up some other**
> **way, the same is a thief and a robber.**
> **But he that *entereth in by the door* is the shepherd of**
> **the sheep.**
>
> **John 10:1,2**

This passage illustrates the difference between the devil's path
to stolen authority and the legal path God used to bring Jesus, the
Prince of Peace and the Great Shepherd, to the throne as Lord of
lords and King of kings.

The "sheepfold" in this passage may be seen as the earth and the
realm of mankind. You have to be *born* into this world to have authority in this realm. There is no such thing as a "naturalized citizen"
where mankind and the spirit realm are concerned. You have to be an
eternal spirit born in the flesh to get a human body and enjoy the full
range of expression you ought to have.

Jesus Was Referring to the "Door of Birth"

When Jesus said, "He that entereth not by the door into the
sheepfold." He was referring to the "door" of birth from a mother's
womb. This was the legal path God the Son would have to take to
legally enter the sheepfold of our world.

Jesus said that anyone who enters the sheepfold of the world by
any other way than through the door of birth from a mother's womb
was "a thief and a robber." He clearly separated Himself from the thief
and robber later in John 10 when He said:

> I am come that they might have life, and that they
> might have it more abundantly.
>> I am the good shepherd: the good shepherd giveth
> his life for the sheep.
>
> John 10:10,11

Remember that Jesus said, "He that entereth in by the door is the shepherd of the sheep" (John 10:2). Only one heavenly Being came into our world through natural birth. There was only One who was born of the woman, and now He is the Great Shepherd of the sheep of God. "The Lord is my shepherd, I shall not want" (Psalm 23:1).

In Jesus, God fulfilled His prophetic declaration to Satan in Genesis 3:15: "The seed of the woman shall bruise thy head!" According to the "Greatly Amplified and Excited Butler Paraphrase," The seed of the woman will put His foot on your head, Satan, and do the mashed potato!"

Satan didn't know the details at the time, but he knew trouble was coming his way some day. He couldn't figure out how God could make good on His promise, because the devil was sure he had mankind and the earth all locked up.

SATAN THOUGHT: *THEY ARE ALL MINE!*

Satan knew that every man and woman who was born on the earth had to have a daddy. He knew that meant that every human being would be born with the nature of death, and he thought, *That means they are mine!* (As I understand it, modern medicine has confirmed that the male always determines the blood type in a baby, and the placental wall separates the blood of the baby from the blood of its mother.)

The good news is that God had a plan for man and for the redemption of the flesh of man that would overturn all of the evil Satan had done!

God in His wisdom ordained that a pure virgin would have a child in the fullness of time. This child would be born *without a natural father* and would thus bypass the "father-to-child" curse that plagued the blood of the human race.

This is why no believer can accept the heretical claim that there was no virgin birth. If there was no virgin birth, then Jesus was born of a natural father and inherited the sin-tainted blood of mankind. That means there would be no legal salvation for mankind.

Praise God, Jesus Christ was born of a virgin. The one called Emmanuel, "God with us," was without sin because he was born of Mary, who "was found with child of the Holy Ghost" (Matt. 1:18).

SATAN SCREAMED, "THAT'S NOT FAIR!"

I can almost hear the great deceiver screaming in anger, "That's not fair!" Oh, but it was legal! Satan usurped the throne of earth as a thief by coming through "another way," but God came to redeem us by entering the sheepfold through the legal doorway of natural birth. Bless God!

Jesus walked the earth as a man born without sin, and for that reason, He was qualified to carry all the sins of mankind on His back. That is why John the Baptist declared with prophetic accuracy, "Behold the Lamb of God, which taketh away the sin of the world" (John 1:29).

God is true to His Word and absolutely and totally just. That meant that He couldn't just step into our world and "do something" in the earth. First He had to find men who would prepare the way by *speaking His Word* into the earth. He had to create the ministry of Jesus long before the Lord ever entered our world in the flesh at Bethlehem. As with everything God does, He did it through His words.

Do you remember the passage quoted earlier from Isaiah 55? God declared that the words He utters never (and that means *never*) return to Him without accomplishing their purpose.

God found a faithful prophet in Isaiah, a bold man who was obedient to speak into the world through his *mouth of flesh* the divine will and purposes of God. In fact, Isaiah delivered more prophecies about the coming Messiah than any other prophet in the Bible.

GOD'S WORD CREATES REALITIES IN THE SEEN REALM

When God needed to get something done, He looked for a man who would fearlessly speak His Word into the earth. Why? That was the only way God was going to see His declared will in heaven accomplished on earth.

God's Word is what creates realities in the seen realm. He launched His plan for the redemption of man by putting His Word *in the mouth of someone who was a legal resident of the earth.*

How does God's Word work in the earth? Isaiah's prophecy reveals some of the inner workings of God's Word in our realm:

> **For as the heavens are higher than the earth, so are my ways higher than your ways, and my thoughts than your thoughts.**
>
> **For as the rain cometh down, and the snow from heaven, and *returneth not* thither, but watereth the earth, and *maketh it bring forth and bud,* that it may give seed to the sower, and bread to the eater:**
>
> **So shall my word be that goeth forth out of my mouth: *it shall not return unto me void, but it shall accomplish that which I please, and it shall prosper* in the thing whereto I sent it.**
>
> **Isaiah 55:9-11**

Satan knew about the dangers of the Word of God. He knew what could happen when God would raise up a man who dared to obey Him and boldly declare God's Word. Satan did everything he could to have God's "mouthpieces" killed and silenced, because once He would put the Word in their mouths and they began to speak the Word in the earth, *there was nothing the devil could do about it.*

Once the Word gets in the earth, it waters the earth. According to the Bible, it actually *makes it bring forth and bud!*

What Word did the Old Testament prophets and John the Baptist speak? They spoke of the One who was coming, the Savior of mankind. Here is just a brief survey of some of the divine Words God planted in the earth through men before Christ came in the flesh:

1. In the garden, God Himself declared the Messiah would be the "seed of the woman" (Gen. 3:15).

2. Isaiah prophesied long after David's death that a leader would come as a child. He said "the government shall be upon his shoulder," and He would bear titles of Wonderful, Counselor, the Mighty God, the Everlasting Father, the Prince of Peace, and His government—upon the throne of David—would never end. (Isa. 9:6,7.)

3. Isaiah also prophesied Jesus' virgin birth and declared His name (or ministry) would be "Emmanuel," meaning "God with us." (Isa. 7:14.)

4. The Lord's birth in lowly Bethlehem was prophesied by Micah the prophet. (Mic. 5:1-5.)

5. Jeremiah the prophet foretold Herod's paranoid massacre of all of the infants in Bethlehem in a failed effort to kill God's chosen deliverer. (Jeremiah 31:15, quoted in Matthew 2:17-18.)

6. The flight of Joseph and Mary with Jesus to Egypt was predicted by Hosea the prophet. (Hos. 11:1.)

7. Isaiah prophesied the coming of the Lord God, who would come like a shepherd to gather and feed His flock. (Isa. 40:10,11.)

8. The prophet Zechariah prophesied of the Lord's betrayal for thirty pieces of silver, and also said His body would be "pierced." (Zech. 11:10,12,13.)

9. Moses learned from God that the Passover Lamb would not have "broken bones." (Ex. 13:2.)

10. David prophesied in detail about the Lord's agony on the cross with His pierced feet and hands, and the prophet

quoted the Lord's "cry of the forsaken" word-for-word. (Ps. 22:1-31.)

11. Isaiah prophesied about Christ's silence before His accusers, of His death between sinners and His burial in a rich man's tomb. (Isa. 53:7,9,12.)

12. David prophesied that God's "Holy One" would be raised from the dead. (Psa. 16:10.)

Every time a man began to speak God's creative Word into the vacuum of man's existence in the Old Testament, Satan tried to kill that prophetic voice. Most of the Old Testament prophets and John the Baptist in the New Testament died for speaking the Word of the Lord, but God's purposes always prevailed. He kept raising up more prophets who kept declaring God's unfailing Word.

They declared where the Messiah would live and how He would die. They described what He would be wearing and how men would gamble for His clothing one day. They quoted word-for-word what He would say and described exactly how He would redeem us from death and damnation. They clearly declared the devil's defeat and the Lord's total victory, but time and time again Satan failed to perceive the complete message.

Once God found men who were willing to speak His Word in the earth, there was nothing the devil could do. The more they preached, prophesied and declared the truth from heaven, the more Word was released to work in the earth.

Finally, there was so much power released by the spoken Word in the earth that the angel of God was compelled to go to a woman named Mary and say:

> Fear not, Mary: for thou hast found favour with God.
> And, behold, thou shalt conceive in thy womb, and bring forth a son, and shalt call his name Jesus.
> He shall be great, and shall be called the Son of the Highest: and the Lord God shall give unto him the throne of his father David.
>
> Luke 1:30,32

This is how the Word brought forth the ministry of Jesus, and this is how God's Word can bring forth God's will in *your life*. This is God's plan for *you* too. This is God's plan for your flesh. He is *still* looking for men and women who are willing to speak His Word into the earth, who are willing to let Him relate to the world of man through their bodies and see His will be done *on earth as it is in heaven.*

As a redeemed child of God, as a king and priest of the Most High and as a new creature of God's Kingdom, clothed in flesh, your body is your badge of authority in the earth; Christ's blood is your badge of authority in the heavenlies; God's Word is your sword of authority in *both realms.*

In His great love, God allows us to see in Christ what can be accomplished when the Word walks among us. The Word laid hands on the sick! The Word cast out devils! The Word raised the dead! The Word caused the blind to see! The Word washed away our sins! The Word rose from the dead!

GOD'S WORD:
THE MOST POWERFUL FORCE EVER RELEASED!

The most powerful thing in the universe is not some chemical, atomic, nuclear or hydrogen weapon of mass destruction. No, the most powerful force ever released in the history of the universe is the Word of God! God's Word stands forever, and it is the prime creative force of the God who "calleth those things which be not as though they were" (Rom. 4:17). God's Word creates! His Word lives!

I am thankful that Satan wasn't much of a student of prophecy. Satan didn't understand what was happening during the thirty-three years Jesus ministered on the earth. God gave the devil fair warning in Genesis 3:15, but he just didn't get it. Had the princes of this world known, they would have never crucified the Lord of glory.

Satan must have been blind to the prophecies about the death and resurrection of the Redeemer (maybe we shouldn't be surprised—the rabbis and doctors of the Law in Jesus' day were blind to them too). Satan evidently dismissed or didn't know about Jesus' own prophetic declarations about His suffering, His death on a cross and most importantly, His resurrection from the dead three days later.

SATAN: THE VICTIM OF GOD'S MASTER STRATEGY

Satan and his unwitting human allies didn't know it, but they were about to become the victims of God's master strategy, a strategy that twentieth-century boxers would later call the "rope-a-dope" strategy!

Many years ago, the undefeated world heavy-weight boxing champion was a twenty-four year old named George Foreman. Promoters were calling him "the biggest, strongest man on the planet." He was set to defend his title against an aging, gray-haired ex-champion named Muhammad Ali. Las Vegas odd-makers said there was no comparison between the two men, and they predicted the fight would be over in three rounds.

George Foreman stepped into the ring with confidence. He was undefeated and seemingly unstoppable. He launched himself at Muhammad Ali and began throwing haymakers (powerful blows meant to knock out or stun an opponent).

The harder Foreman tried to close the distance between himself and Muhammad so his powerful punches could find their target, the more Muhammad Ali retreated back into the rope and slipped out of his reach.

While Ali kept shifting, dodging and blocking with the elbow and knee, George kept throwing everything he had at his elusive target. Voices at every side shouted, "Throw it at him! Throw it at him! Take him out, George!"

Finally some of Foreman's legendary blows began to find their target and his aged opponent just seemed to bounce off the ropes from the force of impact. The announcer's voice cracked with excitement as he shouted into the microphone, "Ali's taken another hit! And another one, and yet another! How can he take that punishment for much longer?!"

I'VE GOT YOU RIGHT WHERE I WANT YOU

The devil thought he had Jesus right where he wanted Him when the final battle began in the Garden of Gethsemane. He thought he was big, bad and undefeated in the realm of fallen flesh.

All of the religious folks were rooting for him, and Jesus wasn't even fighting back! The devil lined up all of his false witnesses and Satan did his best to hammer Jesus to the mat for the final count. *It couldn't be easier!* he thought. The fight seemed uncontested in the high priest's house and later in Herod's court.

It got even better when Satan had his human associates wound Jesus with the thorny crown and hit Him with the cat-o'-nine-tails whip. He was almost delirious with excitement when he saw the blood running down, but little did he know....

Jesus took their hits, the best shots the devil could deliver. It looked as if He couldn't defend Himself, but God had a plan.

In the Foreman-Ali fight, George began to notice that he was getting tired. In all of his experience in the ring, he didn't know that Muhammad Ali was known more for his brains in the ring than for his brawn. He was the fighter who fought with a plan. Foreman quickly learned that lesson after Muhammad Ali suddenly seemed to come alive! The older fighter bounded off the ropes when the time was right and quickly knocked out his cocky younger opponent in front of a shocked crowd.

SATAN DIDN'T KNOW IT WAS TIME FOR A RESURRECTION

Jesus used the same strategy in the depths of hell on the third day, long before the Foreman-Ali boxing match. Satan had no clue it was time for a resurrection. He didn't know that every drop of blood, every stripe on Jesus' shredded back and every wound on His precious head would bring healing, redemption, deliverance, prosperity and resurrection to God's highest creation.

One minute Satan and his demons were dancing in hideous triumph thinking they had successfully humiliated God by killing and disfiguring His Son; then God the Father's voice shook the gates of hell as He said, "It's enough! It's enough! The claims of justice have been satisfied!" In that cosmic moment of time, Jesus "rebounded off the ropes" and threw off the bounds of the principality of darkness. He decked the devil with an eternal blow and stripped him of the keys of death, hell and the grave!

When all was said and done, Jesus declared, "All power is given unto me in heaven and in earth. Go ye therefore..." (Matt. 28:18,19).

Adam "messed up," but God fixed it up! Adam's sin landed us in the slave market, but God's Son bought us back. Adam made a wrong choice and pulled us all down with its consequences. Jesus made the right choice, and the consequences of His sacrifice pulled us back up into full relationship with our Father in heaven.

God's plan for *your* flesh is summed up in this passage from His Word:

> **I beseech you therefore, brethren, by the mercies of God, that ye *present your bodies* a living sacrifice, holy, acceptable unto God, which is your reasonable service.**
> **Romans 12:1**

Present yourself for service and open your mouth with boldness. It is time to plant God's Word in the earth for a fresh harvest. It is His plan for you.

God's Plan for Your Financial Freedom

God's plan for man is rooted in the rock-solid foundation of His Word. He has given us a vast storehouse of divine promises, declarations of His will in certain circumstances and detailed accounts of His faithfulness from generation to generation.

The area of finances and the provision of our needs seems to dominate the body of promises recorded in the Bible, a fact that must irritate my brethren who feel Christians shouldn't talk about money in church.

It seems to me that we are obligated to talk about the things God talks about in His Word. If He talks about finances or righteousness a great deal of the time, then so should we.

God touched on the most important of all the principles of Kingdom economics when He told Adam in the Garden of Eden, "Behold, I have given you every herb bearing seed, which is upon the face of all the earth, and every tree, in the which is the fruit of a tree yielding seed; to you it shall be for meat" (Gen. 1:29).

The phrase "herb bearing seed" in the Hebrew means "seeding seed," which is different in purpose and quality from other seeds. When a farmer plants an acre of corn, he waits patiently for the time of harvest to come, and then he harvests the corn.

In the days before farmers started to buy their "seeding seed" from seed companies each year, a farmer would do one thing before he did anything else with his harvested crop. He would closely examine the crop and search for the very best stalks and the very best ears of corn. Once he had separated these top samples, he set them aside for a special purpose.

All of the rest of the crop could be sold at market or eaten by his family until the next crop came in, but not the "seeding seed." Our term for it is "seed corn," because the farmer reserved these top-performing corn seeds as the corn he would plant in the ground for his next growing season.

SEED CORN REPRESENTS THE BOUNTY OF YOUR NEXT HARVEST

This is a principle for life: You always set aside your best as seed corn. When you plant your best strains of corn the following year, the chances are good that your entire crop will manifest the same superior growth and seed production qualities as the seed corn it came from. Seed corn represents the full bounty of your next harvest, only it is in seed form.

When you take the best that you have and replant it, it gives you a greater yield. This is how God describes your tithes and offerings.

Your tithe is your seeding seed. God said, "I want the very best." You don't eat your tithe, because it too represents the full bounty of your next harvest of God's blessings and provision in *seed form*. You plant your best so you can reap a higher-yield harvest the next season.

God said something else about the "seeding seed" that sounds strange to modern ears: "...to you it shall be for meat" (Gen. 1:29). He was telling Adam in plain terms that he would live by what that "seeding seed" produced. It was God's plan for man. God gave man the seed corn, and man was responsible for using God's gift of seed wisely.

Nothing has changed. Even God submitted Himself to this principle: He planted His Son in the earth and let Him die so He could reap a great harvest of sons and daughters through Christ.

JOIN YOUR FAITH WITH YOUR "WORKS"

Remember that the promises of God are not "activated" merely by *hearing* them. They are not even activated solely by having faith that they are true. The promises of God are activated when *faith is joined with "works."* In other words, God's Word works for *doers* of the Word, but not for those who only *hear* the Word and fail or refuse to act on it.

Jesus also taught us about the law of sowing and reaping, and He applied it to every area of life—specifically including the financial area. In the gospel of Luke, He delivered to His disciples what we have come to call "the Beatitudes" and "the Similitudes." Toward the end of His message, He said:

> **Give, and it shall be given unto you; good measure, pressed down, and shaken together, and running over, shall men give into your bosom. For with the same measure that ye mete withal it shall be measured to you again.**
>
> **Luke 6:38**

This is a picture of the way grain or produce is dispensed to buyers at open-air markets to this day. There were no cash registers or prepackaged foods with pre-measured amounts in Jerusalem in Jesus' day, and they are still absent from most of the open-air markets in many nations today.

It is a rare sight to see a vendor in an open-air market pour your grain into a container on a weigh scale until it runs over. It is rarer still to see them press it down as firmly as possible and pour on *more* until it runs over again!

You will *never* see someone do all of these things and then *shake down* the contents of the container and pour in more until it runs over again. This is the kind of return Jesus *promised* to believers who *give* without measure. If you noticed, Jesus said plainly that *men* would provide these blessings to us!

The apostle Paul restated the principle of reaping and sowing in a way that is clear and understandable for nearly everyone:

> **But this I say, He which *soweth sparingly* shall *reap also sparingly;* and he which *soweth bountifully* shall *reap also bountifully.***

Every man according as he purposeth in his heart, so let him give; not grudgingly, or of necessity: *for God loveth a cheerful giver.*

And God is able to make all grace abound toward you; that ye, always having all sufficiency in all things, may abound to every good work:

(As it is written, He hath dispersed abroad; he hath given to the poor: his righteousness remaineth for ever.

Now he that ministereth *seed to the sower* both minister bread for your food, and *multiply your seed sown,* and *increase the fruits of your righteousness;)*

Being enriched in every thing to all bountifulness, *which causeth through us thanksgiving to God.*

2 Corinthians 9:6-11

The law of reaping and sowing, of seedtime and harvest, is at work in everyone's life, whether they know it or believe in it or not.

THE PRINCIPLES OF SOWING AND REAPING WORK FOR EVERYBODY

There are three ways to respond to this eternal law. You can go through life blindly and without direction, living as a "pawn" at the mercy of hand-me-downs, employers and circumstances, as most people do.

Secondly, you can simply work the divine pattern of increase like any non-believing investor. The *principles* behind God's laws work for non-Christians just as well as they work for Christians.

If you are careful to sow money into a good investment or company, you will surely reap a tidy financial profit from that investment. If you invest yourself in your children, you will reap a rich harvest in your children's lives and in your latter years.

171

If you save money and then invest it wisely, you may well become wealthy. If you sow kindness into the lives of others, you will surely reap kindness somewhere along the road of life.

There is nothing earthshaking or radical about these things, and most non-Christians know about these principles and faithfully operate in them. Most, if not all, of the wealthy people on this planet are benefiting from the "up side" of the basic law of sowing and reaping (although a good number of them will "reap" a very unpleasant consequence for some of their unethical choices in life as well).

GOD'S *BLESSINGS* ARE RESERVED FOR PEOPLE OF FAITH

The third response to God's law of sowing and reaping is to act on God's Word *in faith*. Pay close attention at this point, because we are about to discuss something that is unique and is specifically reserved for people of faith.

When you accept God's Word as divine revelation and act on it, without reservation, as absolute truth, the "simple" law of sowing and reaping ceases to be merely a "system." When you *act* on God's *logos*, or written Word, by *faith,* the *logos* becomes a divine *rhema,* or living revelation, from God to you.

We have already noted that any unsaved person—and I mean *anyone*—can operate according to the principles of the law of sowing and reaping and enjoy significant increase in whatever they sow.

However, *only born-again believers* can sow *with faith* in God's Word and *energize the resources of heaven* on their behalf!

When a believer commits all that he or she does to the Lord, then every time something is sown—whether it is money, time, resources, forgiveness, assistance for others or your hopes for the future—God considers it to be an open declaration of faith in His Word!

YOU CHALLENGE GOD EVERY TIME YOU GIVE IN FAITH

Do you find it hard to believe? Your faith, combined with the risk it takes to act on that faith, literally release His blessings in heaven. In fact, it even *raises a challenge* to Him to once again prove what He declared through the prophet Malachi, and it is a challenge He loves to meet time and time again:

> Bring ye all the *tithes* into the storehouse, that there may be meat in mine house, and *prove me* now herewith, saith the Lord of hosts, if *I will not open you the windows of heaven, and pour you out a blessing, that there shall not be room enough to receive it.*
>
> And I will rebuke the devourer for your sakes, and he shall not destroy the fruits of your ground; neither shall your vine cast her fruit before the time in the field, saith the Lord of hosts.
>
> And all nations shall call you *blessed:* for ye shall be a delightsome land, saith the Lord of hosts.
>
> Malachi 3:10-12

A life lived for God's glory and pleasure is a life immersed in the unlimited favor, blessings and provision of God Himself. He loves a "giving contest." I believe when He finds a cheerful giver who dares to believe everything He has declared in the Word, He gets excited about once again proving His Word to one of His children!

At this point you may be thinking, *Wait a minute! What happened to the sold-out life of a disciple we see in the gospels? If this is the way it's supposed to be, why didn't we see Jesus and Paul living in prosperity?* These are legitimate questions that deserve straight-forward answers.

First of all, we need to understand that money, in and of itself, is not evil. The Scriptures do not say that money is evil; they say, "For the *love* of money is the root of all evil: which while some coveted after, they have erred from the faith, and pierced themselves through with many sorrows" (1 Tim. 6:10). The Greek word translated as "love" in this verse means "avarice, covetous lust for silver."[1]

Secondly, God loves to bless His children, but the highest service we can offer Him is to follow in the sacrificial footsteps of Jesus, who laid down His life for others.

JESUS DID NOT HAVE A "POVERTY SPIRIT"

We know that Jesus was lowly in spirit, but He did not have a "poverty spirit." He wore a seamless outer garment, or coat, that was so highly prized that the Roman guards at the foot of the cross openly gambled for the right to claim it as their own. (John 19:23,24.) We also know that the needs of the group following Jesus were underwritten by the generous donations of wealthy women who also followed Him when He was near their home towns. (Luke 8:2,3.)

It is conceivable that Paul could have lived a long and comfortable life while teaching the Word and evangelizing, but he willingly chose to go to face probable death in Jerusalem when warned by the Holy Spirit of his imminent captivity. (Acts 21:10-13.) Why? He loved his Jewish countrymen so much that he was willing to lay down his life in a last-ditch effort to reach them with the gospel of the Messiah.

We also know that Paul could have received financial support from congregations who looked to him for leadership. He noted that Peter and the other apostles did just that and they were within their rights to do so. (1 Cor. 9:5-12.)

However, Paul *chose* instead to work with his own hands to pay his way and the way of the young men traveling with him to further his apostolic church-planting ministry in unevangelized regions. (Acts 20:33,34.) Paul wanted to make sure that the unsaved people he met would have no chance to even accuse him of "having financial strings" (or a profit motive) attached to his gospel.

Many outreach ministries today who are called to reach the lost in impoverished areas take the same measures so there will be no cultural misunderstandings. If the people they want to reach live in mud huts, they live in mud huts. This is good and acceptable in the sight of God.

NEARLY EVERY MISSIONARY OUTREACH IS SUPPORTED BY GIVERS

Remember that outreach efforts to unreached people groups are almost always expensive. Nearly every one of these important missionary outreach ministries is underwritten by the generous financial support of prospering Christians in other lands.

The New Testament contains many warnings and words of correction aimed at the wealthy. In every case, the problem being addressed is their excessive love for money, almost as if it had become an idol in their lives. No man is to trust in money for anything. The apostle Paul told Timothy:

> **Charge them that are rich in this world, that they be not highminded, nor trust in uncertain riches, but in the living God, who giveth us richly all things to enjoy;**
> **That they do good, that they be rich in good works, ready to distribute, willing to communicate;**
> **Laying up in store for themselves a good foundation against the time to come, that they may lay hold on eternal life.**
>
> **1 Timothy 6:17-19**

God put "wealth" in the proper perspective once and for all when He said: "But thou shalt remember the Lord thy God: for it is he that giveth thee power to get wealth, that he may establish his covenant which he sware unto thy fathers, as it is this day" (Deut. 8:18).

What is this "covenant which he sware unto thy fathers"? The answer is found in the book of Deuteronomy, and it is the foundation for much of what Jesus and the apostles taught about finances in the New Testament.

A SLAVERY MENTALITY SETS YOU UP FOR FAILURE

I have little patience with people who whine to me about how the legacy of slavery in the United States has robbed the

African American of any fair chance to get ahead and succeed in life. I totally agree that slavery was and is wrong. I also agree that *slavery mentality* can set anyone up for failure—if you allow it to.

African Americans suffered under the tyranny of organized slavery in America for about 200 years and have had to live with the lingering after-effects of racial prejudice into the present day. As an African American man, I can tell you it isn't easy. *But,* and this a *big but:* In Christ, *all things are new.* (See 2 Corinthians 5:17.)

The Jews suffered under the forced-labor slavery of Egypt for a full 400 years before they were delivered through the ministry of Moses. It took them 40 miserable years and the death of an entire generation to escape the mental chains of the *slave mentality* they acquired during their stay in Egypt.

It is time for every born-again believer, regardless of their color, race or history, to strip off every last shred of that devilish bondage.

YOU ARE FREE INDEED!

According to the Bible, Jesus said, "If the Son therefore shall make you free, ye shall be free indeed" (John 8:36). You can either believe what the devil wants you to believe, or you can believe the truth of God's Word.

Make your choice, and live with the consequences. Once again we find ourselves confronted by God's law of sowing and reaping.

Anyone and everyone who is willing to hear the Word of the Lord and apply it in their lives by faith can prosper. I don't care whether you live in an exclusive Manhattan apartment or a slum unit in the Watts District of Los Angeles: God's Word is as true for you as it is for me. Believe and act on it by faith, and you will prosper.

God prophesied these words to the Israelites through Moses just before his death, and before they crossed the river Jordan into the Promised Land: "I call heaven and earth to record this day against you, that I have set before you life and death, blessing and cursing: therefore choose life, that both thou and thy seed may live" (Deut. 30:19).

EXAMINE GOD'S PROMISES TO ABRAHAM

No discussion of "kingdom economics" is complete without a thorough examination of God's promises to Abraham and his descendants in Deuteronomy 28.

Many critics of the biblical teaching that God wants to bless us protest that the divine blessings promised to Abraham in Deuteronomy 28 were meant to apply to the Jews only, and not to Gentile, or non-Jewish, people.

I have to confess that I don't have an answer *of my own.* I don't need one. God's Word answers this challenge for me:

> **That *the blessing of Abraham* might *come on the Gentiles through Jesus Christ*; that we might receive the promise of the Spirit through faith.**
>
> **Galatians 3:14**

I don't think I need to explain the meaning of that verse, so we can go on to what God has to say about the blessings He wants to give to everyone who listens to His voice and obeys His Holy Word:

> **And it shall come to pass, if thou shalt hearken diligently unto the voice of the Lord thy God, to observe and to do all his commandments which I command thee this day, that the Lord thy God will set thee on high above all nations of the earth:**
>
> **And** *all these blessings shall come on thee, and overtake thee, if* **thou shalt hearken unto the voice of the Lord thy God.**
>
> **Deuteronomy 28:1,2**

The list of divine blessings we are about to examine aren't "passive promises." Once you activate them by faith accompanied by works, these blessings will actually chase you down and overtake you!

I am not the one saying these things. If you have a problem with them, you'll have to talk to God about it! Just read through these blessings in God's Word and let them soak deep into your mind and spirit!

If you ever really wondered what God thinks about whether or not His people should receive blessings, favor and prosperity, read on:

> **And** *all these blessings shall come on thee, and overtake thee, if* **thou shalt hearken unto the voice of the Lord thy God.**
>
> *Blessed shalt thou be in the city, and blessed shalt thou be in the field.*
>
> *Blessed shall be the fruit of thy body, and the fruit of thy ground, and the fruit of thy cattle, the increase of thy kine, and the flocks of thy sheep.*

Blessed shall be thy basket and thy store.

Blessed shalt thou be when thou comest in, and blessed shalt thou be when thou goest out.

The Lord shall cause thine enemies that rise up against thee to be smitten before thy face: they shall come out against thee one way, and flee before thee seven ways.

The Lord shall command the blessing upon thee in thy storehouses, and in all that thou settest thine hand unto; and he shall bless thee in the land which the Lord thy God giveth thee.

The Lord shall establish thee an holy people unto himself, as he hath sworn unto thee, if thou shalt keep the commandments of the Lord thy God, and walk in his ways.

And all people of the earth shall see that thou art called by the name of the Lord; and they shall be afraid of thee.

And the Lord shall make thee plenteous in goods, in the fruit of thy body, and in the fruit of thy cattle, and in the fruit of thy ground, in the land which the Lord sware unto thy fathers to give thee.

The Lord shall open unto thee his good treasure, the heaven to give the rain unto thy land in his season, and to bless all the work of thine hand: and *thou shalt lend unto many nations, and thou shalt not borrow.*

And the Lord shall make thee the head, and not the tail; and thou shalt be above only, and thou shalt not be beneath; if that thou hearken unto the commandments of the Lord thy God, which I command thee this day, to observe and to do them.

Deuteronomy 28:2-13

John the apostle sums up God's will concerning your finances when he declares, "Beloved, I wish above all things that thou mayest prosper and be in health, even as thy soul prospereth" (3 John 1:2).

Jesus goes one step further to bring a divine balance to our understanding of God's provision. He warns us not to be anxious about material things, especially the basic things we *need* for life.

Many people don't realize that God promises to *automatically* supply our needs. He delights in pouring out His blessings over and above our needs, but first our obedience and purity of heart are required:

> No man can serve two masters: for either he will hate the one, and love the other; or else he will hold to the one, and despise the other. Ye cannot serve God and mammon.
>
> Therefore I say unto you, *Take no thought for your life, what ye shall eat, or what ye shall drink; nor yet for your body, what ye shall put on.* Is not the life more than meat, and the body than raiment?
>
> Behold the fowls of the air: for they sow not, neither do they reap, nor gather into barns; yet your heavenly Father feedeth them. Are ye not much better than they?
>
> Which of you by taking thought can add one cubit unto his stature?
>
> And why take ye thought for raiment? Consider the lilies of the field, how they grow; they toil not, neither do they spin:
>
> And yet I say unto you, That even Solomon in all his glory was not arrayed like one of these.
>
> Wherefore, if God so clothe the grass of the field, which to day is, and to morrow is cast into the oven, shall he not much more clothe you, O ye of little faith?
>
> Therefore take no thought, saying, What shall we eat? or, What shall we drink? or, Wherewithal shall we be clothed?
>
> (For after all these things do the Gentiles seek:) for your heavenly Father knoweth that ye have need of all these things.
>
> Matthew 6:24-36

There is no better way to end this chapter on God's plan for your financial freedom than with the words of Jesus:

> But *seek ye first* the kingdom of God, and his righteousness; and *all these things shall be added* unto you.
> Take therefore no thought for the morrow: for the morrow shall take thought for the things of itself.
> Matthew 6:33,34

God's Plan for Health and Healing:
The Sabbath Rest and the Healing Word

Sickness and disease. Pain and suffering. It almost hurts just to read these words or say them out loud, doesn't it? It should. These things do not exist in the place you came from and the place you are going.[1]

God created the earth as the perfect environment for the human race, and it seems that He created the human body to last forever. When sin came, so did the genetic mutations that simply imitated in the body what had happened in the spirit of man.

Instead of choosing what is right, instead of choosing to work together, the DNA in the cells of the human body duplicated on a cellular level what Adam and Eve did on a spiritual level—they chose to "go their own way" instead of the way intended by the Creator.

As part of the curse, the environment became harsh and hostile to the human race. Some believing scientists point to the significant changes in the human life span recorded in the Bible, and say something happened to the atmosphere after the Great Flood that allowed harmful levels of ultra-violet light to enter the atmosphere. This contributed to even more degradation of the human DNA and shortened life spans.

The physical degradation of the human race was nothing compared to what happened to our "inner man." Most of the pain and suffering experienced by people today isn't caused by sickness and disease; it can be traced to the actions of people who prey on others.

WE ARE SAVED "TO THE BONE," NOT JUST THE SOUL

God did more than provide a cure for our spiritual sickness through a Savior: He also provided a cure for our physical sickness, and it is all wrapped up and contained in Jesus Christ.

The Psalmist declared with prophetic authority:

> **Then they cry unto the Lord in their trouble, and he saveth them out of their distresses.**
> *He sent his word, and healed them,* **and delivered them from their destructions.**
>
> **Psalm 107:19,20**

The Hebrew word translated "healed" is *rapha,* and it means "to mend, to cure, to heal, physician, repair thoroughly, make whole." This is the same word God chose to be one of His seven redemptive names—*Jehovah Rapha,* "I Am the Lord That Healeth Thee." (See Exodus 15:26.)

Jesus invaded our world in the flesh as the embodiment of all seven of those holy names. He didn't come to save our souls while leaving our bodies to rot in the cesspool of our fallen world. He brought total salvation. God literally sent His *Word*, His divine *Logos*, the living Jehovah-Rapha, to heal us as well as to redeem us from the curse of sin and death.

WITH EVERY STRIPE, JESUS PURCHASED OUR HEALING

When Jesus submitted His royal back to the whips of His captors, Satan thought it was *his day* to gloat. He didn't realize that every time the flesh-rending cat-o'-nine-tails bit into Jesus' flesh, the Lord was purchasing healing and deliverance for everyone who would ever battle the ravages of cancer, multiple sclerosis, diabetes, chronic emphysema, lupus, cystic fibrosis, leprosy and all other painful or life-threatening sicknesses and diseases.

Every stripe the enemies of God laid on Jesus' back purchased healing for the nations. Isaiah the prophet foretold of the Messiah who would come, saying:

> **But he was wounded for our transgressions, he was bruised for our iniquities: the chastisement of our peace was upon him; and *with his stripes we are healed.***
> **Isaiah 53:5**

This passage is echoed in the New Testament by Peter the apostle in his epistle to the churches in 1 Peter 2:24. Nothing seems to challenge our Christian faith as much as sickness and disease. A biblical approach to these challenges immediately isolates us from most of the world, including most medical doctors and scientists. It doesn't have to be this way, but it usually is.

ALL MEDICAL AND SCIENTIFIC KNOWLEDGE COMES FROM GOD

I understand that many of the great advances in the practice of medicine and the healing arts were produced by devout Christians who saw no conflict between their faith in the healing God and the application of scientific and medical principles to the treatment of human disease.

They understood that all such knowledge ultimately comes from God, either by revelation or through the intelligence and mandate of dominion God gave mankind in the beginning. I still believe that way.

Sadly, I've noticed that most of the people who criticize the belief that God heals today are *church-going Christians*. Perhaps they look at the flood of disease and sickness in the world and conclude that healing *cannot* be part of the redemptive package. My question is this: What does God have to say about healing and health in His Word?

Circumstances and personal experience *must* take a backseat to God's Word.

Evangelist F.F. Bosworth takes us back to the same foundation in a powerful book he wrote in 1924 entitled *Christ the Healer: Sermons on Divine Healing*. His ministry was noted for the way God healed and worked astounding signs and wonders in his meetings.

Bosworth presents a solid scriptural groundwork for divine healing in his book that has been echoed by many of the great healing ministries in the years that have followed.

I want to share several paragraphs from his book that clearly describe God's plan for man in the areas of health and healing. Concerning the question, "Is healing in God's will for us today?" Rev. Bosworth wrote:

> For the answer to the question under consideration, let us look away from modern tradition and go to the Word of God, which is a revelation of His will.
>
> In the 15th chapter of Exodus, just after the passage of the Red Sea, which typified our redemption, and "was written for our admonition," God gave His first promise to heal. This promise was for *all*. God named the conditions, the conditions were met, and we read: "He brought them forth also with silver and gold, and there was not one feeble person among all their tribes." It is here that God gave the covenant of healing, revealed by and sealed with His first covenant and Redemptive name, *Jehovah-Rapha*, translated, "I am the Lord that healeth thee." This is God's word, "settled in heaven," a never-changing fact concerning God.

WHO IS AUTHORIZED TO CHANGE GOD'S WILL?

> To say that this privilege of health is not for God's people today, is to change God's "I *Am*" to "I *Was*" Jehovah-Rapha. Who has the authority to change God's Redemptive names? Instead of abandoning His office as Healer, He is "Jesus Christ, the same yesterday, today, and forever," under this first covenant name, as well as under the other six. The blessings revealed by His Redemptive names...were provided by the Atonement, when He "tasted death *for every man*," and therefore cannot be confined to Israel.[2]

187

You may be battling for your physical life as you read these words. I encourage you to think of your Redeemer tied to a post as sweaty soldiers took turns swinging a bloody whip toward His precious back.

Every stripe that was cut into His flesh became a *cure* for your sickness! Every wound He suffered at the hands of man became a healing balm in God's hand for *you*—the exact divine prescription of divine health and wholeness for you today.

It is God's plan and will for you to apply every stripe on His back to the sickness or disease afflicting your body! While Satan thought his triumph was complete, Jesus knew that every stripe would make His Father's plan for man's redemption complete by extending His grace beyond the spirit and the soul to include every cell of our bodies!

What is God's attitude toward our physical health and healing today? Did it all pass away when Jesus was laid in the grave? Did it pass away with the apostles of the first century? Hardly. We don't have to guess or make conjectures about God's position toward physical healing. He stated it for us through John the apostle:

> **Beloved, I wish above all things that thou mayest prosper *and be in health*, even as thy soul prospereth.**
>
> **3 John 1:2**

As for healing, its administration was *never reserved* for the apostles according to the Scriptures. From the very beginning of the church, God used average believers and deacons as well as apostles to deliver healing to hurting or diseased bodies.

We know He used Peter and Paul to minister healing, but we sometimes forget about how He used a deacon named Stephen to dramatically heal the sick. (See Acts 6:5-8.) When the 120 were waiting and praying for the advent of the Holy Spirit in the upper room, the room was shaken *after* they prayed:

> **And now, Lord, behold their threatenings: and grant unto thy servants, that with all boldness they may speak thy word,**
>
> **By *stretching forth thine hand to heal*; and that *signs and wonders may be done* by the name of thy holy child Jesus.**
>
> Acts 4:29,30

God also called and anointed the *entire body of Christ* to pray the prayer of faith for the sick, linked closely with right relationships in His Word: "Confess your faults one to another, and pray one for another, that ye may be healed. The effectual fervent prayer of a righteous man availeth much" (James 5:16).

CAN THERE BE ANY DOUBT THAT GOD STILL HEALS?

Then He distributes supernatural *gifts of healings* to various members of His body "as the Spirit wills" to help maintain the health of the body and as a sign and wonder to those who do not believe. (See 1 Corinthians 12:7-11.) Can there be any doubt that *Jehovah-Rapha* is still in the healing business?

Our brief discussion of God's plan for health and healing cannot end without a return to God's original plan for man in the book of Genesis. Many of our health problems can be traced to our ignorance or dismissal of the "day of rest principle" in Genesis:

> And on the seventh day *God ended his work* which he had made; and *he rested* on the seventh day from all his work which he had made.
> And *God blessed the seventh day,* and *sanctified it:* because that in it he had rested from all his work which God created and made.
>
> Genesis 2:2,3

THE SABBATH PRINCIPLE WAS ESTABLISHED FOR MAN

God blessed the seventh day and sanctified it, or "set it apart." While the Jews were required to observe the seventh day, presumably Saturday, as a holy sabbath, Jesus gave us a clearer understanding of the sabbath principle. He said, "The sabbath was made for man, and not man for the sabbath" (Mark 2:27).

Paul added that godliness doesn't consist of observing sabbath days. (See Colossians 2:16-17.) The point is that God established the sabbath, or "day of rest" principle for man's own good.

God "worked" for six days and rested on the seventh as an example for His creation. Man was not made to work seven days straight. We can work for six days, but somehow, some way, we have to set aside a day for rest. The best way to spend that day is to devote it to fellowship with the saints and worship and meditation toward God.

GOD WON'T "GET US"—OUR BODIES WILL!

If we violate the "day of rest principle," we will pay the consequences in our physical bodies. No, God won't "get us" for violating some religious sabbath rule. Our bodies will "get us" for violating and abusing them. The effects of overwork and physical abuse usually don't show up right away, but even in our work patterns we are subject to the eternal law of sowing and reaping!

If you sow abuse to your physical body by ignoring the "day of rest principle" instituted by God, then you will reap sickness, disease and accelerated aging. It is that simple. No matter how much faith and power you think you have, they will not assist your choice to bypass God's plan for maximum health.

I won't go into the importance of a wise and balanced diet of healthy foods in moderation, and of regular exercise; but you know they are necessary. God won't punish us for abuse in these areas, but we can't blame Him if our choices cause us to show up at heaven's gates earlier than He planned due to sickness or disease!

If you have already skipped sabbaths for twenty years, eaten too many barbecue dinners and too few vegetables and helped underwrite the annual cookie fund-raisers for hundreds of Girl Scouts over the years, repent and commit the sin of excess work and "too much, too often" no more. Apply the truths of God's biblical plan for health and healing from this day forward.

In health, as in every area of life, God has a plan for you that will cause you to prosper—if you follow it.

God's Plan for You

God sowed three great "seed-bearing seeds" into this planet. The *first* seed was the seed of His own breath invested in a mound of dirt He had carefully formed with His own hands. The result was the creation of an eternal creature named Adam, made in God's own image and after His likeness. You are directly descended from that first man and father.

The second and greatest "seed-bearing seed" God ever planted (I said *planted,* not *created*) was Jesus Christ, His only begotten Son. For reasons we described earlier, God sent His Son in the form of a baby born to a virgin, and He "planted" His Son, the living Word, in the earth.

God did this knowing that His divine seed-bearing Seed was destined to be replanted in the earth in "death" and would rise again to produce a harvest of sons and daughters for eternity.

The third "seed-bearing seed" God planted can actually be traced to the first two seeds, but I'll trace it back to the Day of

Pentecost when the Holy Spirit descended on the 120 in the Upper Room in Jerusalem as God promised.

In that moment, the Holy Spirit descended and filled those believers with the abiding, indwelling presence of God; and the Church of Jesus Christ was born. God was doing a new thing; a fresh bud bloomed in the midst of man's spiritual desert. (See Isaiah 43:18-19.)

HE HAS GIVEN YOU POWER AND DOMINION— *NOW WHAT?*

You are the fruit of God's "sowing and reaping" since the beginning of time. You are a child of God, destined and ordained to rule and reign through Christ. He has given you the keys of the kingdom and the power of dominion through His Word. *Now what happens?*

Just before Jesus took His last breath on the cross of Calvary, He said to the Father, "It is *finished*" (John 19:30). He meant what He said. His part was complete; now it was time to pass the spiritual baton to His spiritual "offspring."

In His last moments on the earth, Jesus looked at the eleven men who had followed Him to the cross and beyond and said:

> **All power is given unto me in heaven and in earth. *Go ye....***
>
> **Matthew 28:18,19**

In other words, Jesus told them, "It's up to you now. I've done My part; now *you do yours.*" He expects—He *believes*—you will follow in His footsteps and do the work of the ministry in the earth.

Jesus was not only the living "Word Incarnate," but He was also a *preacher* of the Word, a *teacher* of the Word, a *speaker* of the Word, a *believer* of the Word; and above all, He was a *doer* of the Word. What are you?

Everything Jesus said, did and was—everything about Him—was literally wrapped up in God's eternal Word. His life was a living illustration of His response to Satan's temptation: "It is written, Man shall not live by bread alone, but by every word that proceedeth out of the mouth of God" (Matt. 4:4).

JESUS SOUGHT HEAVENLY RHEMA TO GUIDE HIS EARTHLY STEPS

Jesus' steps each day fully conformed to the messianic prophecies revealed in the Law and the prophets. He spent time alone with His Father, sometimes praying all night long to receive a fresh *rhema,* or living word, from heaven to guide His steps and actions on earth the following day. Can we say the same thing about our lives?

For good reason, Jesus is called the author and pioneer of our faith. He went to great lengths to willingly lay down the powers and privileges of His divinity while on the earth to show us how we, as ordinary men and women, can live according to God's plan for man in *this life.*

God's plan for man is laid out for us in black and white in the body of the Scriptures. He even went so far as to personally *demonstrate the God-kind-of-life* in the flesh through the life, ministry, sacrificial death and resurrection of Jesus.

His Word provides clear guidelines for our marriages, our families, our friendships and our reason for living. He has revealed every trick in Satan's worn-out book, and He gave us supernatural weapons and authority to overcome the enemy at every turn. He purchased our freedom with His own life, and He purchased our healing with His own blood.

WE ARE BACK IN THE GARDEN FACING A CHOICE...

Once again we find ourselves in the garden, faced with a choice. We can choose to follow God's plan and "have it all," or we can follow our own plan and lose it all. As for "me and my house," we've made our choice. I've done my part by sharing in this book what I feel is God's heart.

Every time I study God's Word and realize how vast His provisions and promises are, I remember the words we read in an earlier chapter, the statements Moses made to the remnant children of Israel just before they crossed the Jordan:

> **I have set before you life and death, blessing and cursing: therefore choose life, that both thou and thy seed may live:**
> **That thou mayest love the Lord thy God, and that thou mayest obey his voice, and that thou mayest cleave unto him: for he is thy life, and the length of thy days: that thou mayest dwell in the land....**
> **Deuteronomy 30:19,20**

Despite their many flaws and failures, God used the Israelites to deliver the Messiah to a lost world. *Now He wants to use you and* me, as the Church of Jesus Christ, to cause His will to be done on earth as it is in heaven.

It is time to follow God's plan with boldness, turning neither to the left nor to the right. This is the time for us to go forth with "a miracle in our mouths" and the creative force of faith in our hearts.

Having offered up our bodies as living sacrifices to God, we have no choice but to "go forth and do great exploits" for our God in our generation. *All we have to do is follow God's plan for man.*

Endnotes

Chapter 2

[1] See John 14:16,17,26; 15:26; 16:7-14.

[2] We will deal with this in greater detail in Chapter 7. To study how Jesus dealt with the temptation of Satan in the wilderness, see Matthew 4:4,6,7,10.

Chapter 3

[1] Strong, "Hebrew," entry #6754.

[2] Strong, "Hebrew," entry #1823.

[3] Strong, "Hebrew," entry #7287.

[4] Strong, "Hebrew," entry #3335.

Chapter 4

[1] Strong, "Hebrew," entry #1129.

[2] Strong, "Hebrew," entry #5828, 5826.

[3] Strong, "Hebrew," entry #5048, 5046.

Chapter 5

[1] Strong, "Hebrew," entry #5647.

[2] *Merriam-Webster's Collegiate Dictionary,* 10th Ed., s.v. "dress."

[3] Strong, "Hebrew," entry #8104.

Chapter 7

[1] Strong, "Hebrew," entry #6175, 6191.

Chapter 8

[1] Strong, "Hebrew," entry #1692.

[2] Strong, "Greek," entry #4722.

Chapter 10

[1] Strong, "Greek," entry #5365.

Chapter 11

[1] You *came* from the presence of God when He gave you life at conception in your mother's womb. You are *going* to heaven, where there are no tears or sorrow, nor sickness or disease.

[2] Strong, "Hebrew," entry #7495.

[3] Bosworth, pp. 37-38.

References

Bosworth, F.F. *Christ the Healer: Sermons on Divine Healing.* Miami Beach, FL: F.F. Bosworth, 1924.

Merriam-Webster's Collegiate Dictionary, Tenth Edition. Springfield, MA: Merriam-Webster, Inc., 1994.

Strong, James. *Strong's Exhaustive Concordance of the Bible.* "Hebrew and Chaldee Dictionary," "Greek Dictionary of the New Testament." Peabody, MA: Hendrickson, n.d.

About the Author

Bishop Keith A. Butler is the founder and senior pastor of Word of Faith International Christian Center.

Word of Faith International Christian Center was founded on January 14, 1979 and is a congregation of 16,000 plus members and 200 employees. The main church is located on a beautiful 110-acre campus in Southfield, Michigan, where multiple services are held in the 5,000 seat auditorium. He also pastors Faith Christian Centers in Smyrna, Georgia, which began in August 1993 and in Phoenix, Arizona, which began in September 1997.

Bishop Butler is a pastor and a Bible teacher with ministerial emphasis on teaching line-by-line and applying God's Word to people's daily lives. He ministers in seminars, conventions and churches throughout the country and in third-world nations.

Bishop Butler has a television ministry called "The Word of Faith," seen nationwide on Black Entertainment Television (BET) and in over fifty countries in Europe.

Bishop Butler is an author and conference speaker who travels all over the world. He and his lovely wife, Deborah, have three children who are all active in the work of the ministry: Pastor and Mrs. Keith A. Butler, II, Minister MiChelle Butler and Ms. Kristina Butler.

You may contact Keith Butler
by writing:

Word of Faith Publications
P.O. Box 3247
Southfield, Michigan 48037-3247

www.wordoffaithicc.org

*Please include
your prayer requests
and comments when you write.*

Other Books by Keith Butler

A Seed Will Meet Any Need

Hell: You Don't Want To Go There!

Success Strategies From Heaven

Angels, God's Servants for You

Available from your local bookstore.

Harrison House

Tulsa, Oklahoma

The Harrison House Vision

Proclaiming the truth and the power

Of the Gospel of Jesus Christ

With excellence;

Challenging Christians to

Live victoriously,

Grow spiritually,

Know God intimately.